Christ, Creeds and Life

Conversations about the
Center of Our Faith

Christ, Creeds and Life

Conversations about the
Center of Our Faith

Edited by

Anne T. Thayer and Douglas Jacobsen

UNITED
CHURCH
PRESS ®

Cleveland

United Church Press, 700 Prospect Avenue, Cleveland, Ohio 44115
unitedchurchpress.com

12   11   10   09   08   07   5   4   3   2   1

Library of Congress Cataloging-in-Publication Data

Christ, creeds and life : conversations about the center of our faith / edited by Anne T. Thayer and Douglas Jacobsen.
   p. cm.
  ISBN 978-0-8298-1766-9 (alk. paper)
  1. Jesus Christ--Person and offices. 2. Creeds. I. Thayer, Anne T. II. Jacobsen, Douglas G. (Douglas Gordon), 1951-
  BT203.C47 2007

Contents

Welcome

Christ, Creeds and Life: Conversations about the Center of Our Faith is written with the goal of helping to spark meaningful discussion about the life and significance of Jesus Christ who is the central focus of our faith. As Christians, we sometimes get so caught up in other activities—either the many time-consuming activities of daily life or the sometimes equally overwhelming busyness of church-related projects and programs—that we lose sight of Christ. The purpose of this book is to help us refocus our attention on Jesus as the founder and sustainer of our faith. As the name of our denomination, United Church of Christ, claims, we are part of the body of Christ—the Christian church. We need to know Jesus Christ in order to live as his disciples.

Four basic questions drive this book: (1) Who is this person, Jesus, on whom our faith is built? (2) What does it mean to identify ourselves as Christ's followers? (3) What do the historic documents of the United Church of Christ say about who Christ is? (4) What relevance does Jesus have for us today?

The point of this little volume is not to provide neat and easy answers to these questions. Our hope is, instead, that thinking about these questions will prompt good conversations with others—conversations that involve both heads and hearts. When those discussions are over we hope everyone involved will not only have learned more about Jesus, but will also have become closer friends with everyone else who has been part of the conversation. While this book can be read alone, it is has quite intentionally been designed for use by small groups where these kinds of life-sharing conversations can take place.

The framework of this study is drawn largely from the United Church of Christ Statement of Faith and the creeds and confessions that constitute the theological heritage of this denomination. As the UCC celebrates its 50th anniversary in 2007 and the 50th anniversary of its Statement of Faith in 2009, it is fitting to commemorate these milestones by looking once again at the documents that have articulated our beliefs about Christ. In addition to the creeds and confessions of the UCC, each chapter also includes pertinent passages from the Bible—the single most important source of information about Christ—as well as excerpts from the songs and liturgies used in weekly worship. Taken together these material documents provide a rich library of resources for reflecting on Christ and his significance for us today.

The UCC has a complex history and deep heritage. The German Reformed and New England Congregational traditions have been especially prominent in that history, but other groups, like the Christian Churches and the German Evangelical Synod, have also contributed particular insights and added depth and breadth to the faith we confess. In this book, we draw on the full wealth of wisdom represented by that mix of traditions, appealing to the catechisms and statements of faith from all these different groups that have coalesced into the UCC. We typically provide only brief citations from these works, but the full texts of most of these documents can be found on the denominational website: www.ucc.org/faith. For an introduction to the history and theology of these statements, we recommend Lee Barrett's Introduction in *The Heidelberg Catechism: A New Translation for the Twenty-first Century* (The Pilgrim Press, 2007).

While two of us have served as editors, this book was produced by all the members of the Theological Commission of the Penn Central Conference of the United

8

Church of Christ working together (see contributor list). What is a "theological commission"? We are a group of ordinary people, some ordained and some not, drawn from the local churches in our region of the country. We usually meet about once a month and our "job" is to reflect on what we are doing and saying as a church. When various social issues crop up we ask what insights the church might have to share on those topics. When controversies arise within a congregation or an association, we are occasionally requested to help clarify what is at stake. We also sometimes ponder general questions like: Are we living up to our ideals as a church? Are we clear about what we believe? How do we currently picture the way of life to which Christ calls us? It was these broader kinds of questions that prompted us a few years ago to begin thinking about how our denomination might help its members better understand the life and meaning of Christ. This book is the result.

Prior to publication, this book was "field tested" in a variety of different settings to make sure the material included was both user-friendly and user-flexible. Everyone knows what "user-friendly" means, but "user-flexible" might require a short explanation. What we mean by "user-flexible" is that every person or group that uses this book should feel free to approach it in whatever way works best for them. There are many different ways to use this book for reflection and study.

As a kind of road map to let you know what is coming, you should know that every chapter is organized basically the same way. The theme of each chapter is drawn from a phrase that appears in the UCC Statement of Faith. An opening section then explains that theme in several short paragraphs and lists several starter questions to get conversation going. Next, a resource section includes relevant verses from the Bible, selected passages from different creeds and confessions of faith, excerpts from the *UCC Book of Worship* relating to the theme, and sample lyrics from songs found in the *New Century Hymnal*. Each chapter then concludes with a section called "Themes for Reflection" (which connects the theme of the chapter to the practice of Christian life today), a set of discussion questions (also designed to help connect the topic to real life), and a closing prayer.

While we have organized the material in each chapter following this format, you should feel free to use it however best suits the needs and style of your group. You may, for example, decide to read the material together, silently or aloud, and then discuss the chapter a section at a time. You may agree to read the materials ahead of time and, during your meeting time, discuss the chapter as a whole or focus mainly on the discussion questions. Some groups may want to divide each chapter in two, discussing the background material one week and the contemporary relevance the next. Or, you may want to reverse the order, starting with the contemporary material and ending up with the creeds and biblical passages. Some groups may want to start by singing a hymn, or by praying the "closing" prayer at the beginning of the time you share together, or by discussing the final discussion questions before you do anything else.

The goal is simply to spark a good and honest conversation about Christ and Christ's continuing significance. The information that we provide is merely a starting point and is not at all exhaustive. Study group participants may want to include other biblical passages, creeds, songs, or prayers that they think will enrich the conversation for everyone. Or, they may want to share other items that have enriched their personal reflection on Christ such as different forms of prayer, works of art, personal experiences, music, short clips of films or television programs, and so on.

The affirmations of the UCC Statement of Faith and the other creeds and confessions that we include are broadly shared by many Christians, not just the UCC, so they help connect us with the church as a whole. But the church is also local—it is the face-to-face gathering of those who receive Christ's gifts and seek to follow Christ's way of life in one particular place—and local expressions of Christian faith are very precious. So incorporate the hymns or repertoire of songs your own congregation uses. Refer to the sections of the *UCC Book of Worship* or other worship resources that your own congregation uses most frequently. Look over your church bulletins and Christian education materials for further examples of what your congregation in particular emphasizes about Christ. Explore your church building to see how Christ is depicted in the artwork that is on display.

You do not need to be an expert to participate in this study, or even to facilitate it! Discussion is central to the process, not expertise. We would encourage all members of the group to share their ideas, even if, on occasion, this might require some restraint on the part of those who are naturally more talkative and some courage on the part of those who are more quiet and shy. Whether your group is a new members' class exploring the faith of the church for the first time or a fellowship group that has been meeting together for years, everyone has something to offer—an insight, a song, or a question.

A previous generation believed much more than we do in simply memorizing the "right answers" to questions about God, Jesus, the Holy Spirit, the church, and the Christian life. "Answers," even if they are right, only get you so far. What is more important is to understand the heritage of our faith in a way that truly transforms our lives. We need to ask ourselves over and over again how Christ is the center of our own living faith, and we need to reflect on how we can explain that living faith to those around us: our children, our friends, our neighbors. This is why conversation is so important. Talking about what we believe with others and explaining how we try to live as followers of Jesus deepens our faith and makes it more real.

In the conversations you have as you read through this book, you will have many different insights to share with others and, no doubt, you will learn much from others as well. We hope that shared learning fosters closer friendships. We also hope that a fresh encounter with these documents from the past will help you feel closer to all those Christians who lived before us and handed the faith down to us. All of us—the Christians of the past and the present—share one common faith that centers on Jesus. It is Jesus Christ who reveals God to us, forgives our sins, heals our wounded spirits, and sets us free to love and serve others. Jesus is and always has been the center of our faith, and Jesus is the focus of this book.

Anne T. Thayer and Douglas Jacobsen

Chapter 1

Studying Christ

Jesus is everywhere in American culture. People wear Jesus t-shirts. He shows up in music videos. Politicians refer to him in their speeches. Hollywood even makes movies about him. But how much do we really know about Jesus? How much do even churchgoing people understand about Christ and Christ's mission in the world?

A popular bumper sticker from several years ago declared, "Jesus is the answer!" Of course, that proclamation quickly called forth the clever retort: "If Jesus is the answer, what is the question?" Bumper stickers are not the best source of truth or insight, but there is something to the question. What do we, as Christians, believe about Jesus and his continuing influence within the world as the risen Christ? What has Christ done for us? What is Christ doing now? What questions does Christ answer for you and me?

The purpose of this book is not to raise every question that could be asked about Christ. That would take forever. Rather it is to explore our understanding of Christ using the theological history and heritage of the United Church of Christ as our guide. What has this denomination, our denomination, had to say about Christ? What passages of the Bible have we as a church found most helpful? What words and phrases about Jesus have shown up most frequently in the liturgies we recite and the songs we sing? Finally, what have our church's official statements of belief—our creeds, confessions, and catechisms—most emphasized about

Christ and Christ's relationship with us and with the world as a whole?

This book is not intended to tell you what you must believe about Jesus. Instead it is a resource designed to prompt good conversation about what our church traditions have taught about Christ in the past, what we proclaim about Christ today, and how Christ really can help answer many of the questions we face every day. We all have something to add to this conversation—ways in which Christ has been and continues to be meaningful to us, favorite images of Christ in art or song, questions about who Jesus really was, and much more—and all of this has a place in the chapters that follow.

Images of Christ in Scripture: A Discussion Exercise

Here's a quick discussion exercise to start things off. Four important New Testament statements about Christ are printed below. Which of these do you find most engaging? Why? Which seems the most strange? What do these passages emphasize about Christ? What else would you want to emphasize about who Christ was and is?

> **John 1:1-4, 14.** In the beginning was the Word, and the Word was with God, and the Word was God. He was in the beginning with God. All things came into being through him, and without him not one thing came into being. What has come into being in him was life, and the life was the light of all people. . . . And the Word became flesh and lived among us, and we have seen his glory, the glory as of a father's only son, full of grace and truth.

> **Acts 10:36-40, 43.** You know the message he sent to the people of Israel, preaching peace by Jesus

Christ—he is Lord of all. That message spread through-out Judea, beginning in Galilee after the baptism that John announced: how God anointed Jesus of Nazareth with the Holy Spirit and with power; how he went about doing good and healing all who were oppressed by the devil, for God was with him. We are witnesses to all that he did both in Judea and in Jerusalem. They put him to death by hanging him on a tree; but God raised him on the third day and allowed him to appear. . . . All the prophets testify about him that everyone who believes in him receives forgiveness of sins through his name.

1 Corinthians 15:3-5. For I handed on to you as of first importance what I in turn had received: that Christ died for our sins in accordance with the scriptures, and that he was buried, and that he was raised on the third day in accordance with the scriptures, and that he appeared to Cephas, then to the twelve.

Ephesians 1:3, 7-10, 13. Blessed be the God and Father of our Lord Jesus Christ, who has blessed us in Christ with every spiritual blessing . . . In him we have redemption through his blood, the forgiveness of our trespasses, according to the riches of his grace that he lavished on us. With all wisdom and insight he has made known to us the mystery of his will, according to his good pleasure that he set forth in Christ, as a plan for the fullness of time, to gather up all things in him, things in heaven and things on earth. . . . In him you also, when you had heard the word of truth, the gospel of your salvation, and had believed in him, were marked with the seal of the promised Holy Spirit.

From the Bible to Creeds to Us

Jesus Christ is at the very center of Christian faith. From the earliest days of the church, believers have focused their proclamation on Jesus of Nazareth who they believed to be the long-awaited Messiah and, indeed, God's fullest self-revelation.

The Bible provides the earliest witness to this remarkable person. The story of Jesus' life on earth is recorded in the four Gospels, each one adding distinctive elements that fill out the portrait of his life. The Gospels tell us what Jesus taught and how he acted, and they also include early accounts of his death and resurrection. The letters in the New Testament reflect what early Christians believed about Jesus: that Christ was sent from God for the purpose of forgiving our sins, liberating us from bondage to the forces of evil, restoring fellowship with God and those around us, and ultimately making all things right. They also reveal how these early Christians encouraged each other to follow Jesus in their daily lives, urging one another to conduct themselves in ways worthy of citizenship in the new spiritual kingdom Jesus inaugurated.

Because the person of Jesus was so central to the Christian faith, the church soon began to formulate its own carefully crafted short statements saying who Christ was. These statements were sometimes used to instruct new believers in the faith of the church in preparation for baptism. They were also used in worship as a means of praising God and of proclaiming the faith that all followers of Christ shared in common. These statements came to be known as confessions of faith or creeds (which comes from the Latin word *credo*, meaning "I believe"). Later many different groups of Christians produced catechisms (short question-and-answer pamphlets), which were used to teach young people the basic Christian beliefs of their various denominations.

The purpose in formulating these statements of faith was never to replace the Bible; instead many of these creeds, confessions, and catechisms were written to answer new questions as they arose within the church. For example, in the early 300s some Christians in Egypt were teaching that Jesus was not fully divine. They said that although Christ was a great being, Christ was a creature and not truly God. In response, church leaders came together and affirmed in the Nicene Creed that Jesus was indeed fully divine, true God from true God.

Many of the most important creeds of the church were written during the fourth through the eighth centuries, and these creeds form a common source of wisdom and insight for all Christians, whether Roman Catholic, Orthodox, or Protestant. A number of other creeds, catechisms, and confessions, many of which have become part of our own UCC heritage, were composed during the Reformations of the 1500s. During this period, the new Protestant denominations were trying to explain exactly how their beliefs either agreed with or differed from the beliefs of the Roman Catholic Church and were developing strategies to pass on the faith from generation to generation. A key question in this period was how exactly Jesus' life, death and resurrection reconcile us with God.

In addition to the knowledge we gain through the Bible and the creeds of the church, Christ is also present with us today through the actions and influence of the Holy Spirit. Our own worship and Christian lives can thus become avenues of access to Jesus. While we continue to follow the one Savior, Jesus Christ whose love for us never changes, we seek to be faithful to that changeless Christ in an ever-changing world. We must therefore reflect carefully not only on what Christ has meant to Christians in centuries past, but also on what Christ is saying to us in the times and places where we live. God is still speaking as the church experiences Christ.

Christ and the Creeds within the UCC

While all three of these sources—the Bible, the creeds, and our own present experience—are used in this study, we give special attention to the historic creeds of our church.

Why study Christ through these creeds and confessions of faith? Because these statements distill the public teaching of the church across the ages and they interpret the witness of the scripture in light of the experience of the church. They represent the best consensus of the church. Along with the Bible, and used in the context of contemporary worship and teaching, these statements provide the skeleton of belief or tradition that gives shape and form to the message of our church.

The United Church of Christ affirms clearly that Jesus Christ is central to our faith and common life. The preamble of the UCC constitution says that we claim as our own "the faith of the historic Church expressed in the ancient creeds and reclaimed in the basic insights of the Protestant Reformers." Thus, when the Evangelical and Reformed Church merged with the Congregational Christian Church to form the UCC in 1957, the creeds and confessions of those older denominations automatically became part of the doctrinal heritage of the UCC.

When the UCC was still a very new denomination, a commission of 30 people was given the task of writing a new statement of faith to give voice to the shared heritage of these merging traditions. The resulting UCC Statement of Faith was adopted in 1959 with great enthusiasm, and was re-issued in the form of a doxology (or hymn of praise addressed to God) in 1981. Its language is evocative rather than definitive, serving as a *testimony* to faith, rather than as a binding *test* of faith. The text of that doxological Statement of Faith reads as follows:

> We believe in you, O God, Eternal Spirit,
> God of our Savior Jesus Christ and our God,
> and to your deeds we testify:
> You call the worlds into being,
> create persons in your own image,
> and set before each one the ways of life and death.
> You seek in holy love to save all people from aimlessness and sin.
> You judge people and nations by your righteous will declared through prophets and apostles.
> In Jesus Christ, the man of Nazareth, our crucified and risen Savior,
> you have come to us and shared our common lot,
> conquering sin and death and reconciling the world to yourself.
> You bestow upon us your Holy Spirit,
> creating and renewing the church of Jesus Christ,
> binding in covenant faithful people of all ages, tongues, and races.
> You call us into your church to accept the cost and joy of discipleship,
> to be your servants in the service of others,
> to proclaim the gospel to all the world and resist the powers of evil,
> to share in Christ's baptism and eat at his table,
> to join him in his passion and victory.

You promise to all who trust you forgiveness of sins
and fullness of grace,
courage in the struggle for justice and peace,
your presence in trial and rejoicing,
and eternal life in your realm which has no end.
Blessing and honor, glory and power be unto you.
Amen.

Most of the chapters in this book take as their main
point of reference one phrase or another from this UCC
Statement of Faith, setting it in the context of scripture and
current worship, and reminding us of the long history of
creedal affirmations we honor as a denomination. Each concludes with themes for reflection and a series of questions
that help connect the older language of the creeds to our
own contemporary lives.

Which Creeds Will We Be Using?
The creeds and confessions that make up the heritage of the
United Church of Christ were written in various times and
places. Although they share much in common, each one
adds a somewhat different nuance. Three of the documents
we will be using were written during the early centuries of
church history:

> **The Apostles' Creed.** Although not actually composed
> by the twelve Apostles, this short statement emerged as
> a baptismal confession used by the early church in
> Rome. In the context of all the gods and goddesses
> available in the Roman Empire, the candidate for bap-
> tism affirmed that he or she was pledging allegiance to
> the one God over all: Father, Son and Holy Spirit.
> Because many in the early centuries found it hard to
> believe that God could truly become human, this creed

stresses Jesus' birth, suffering and death under Pontius Pilate, burial, and resurrection.

The Nicene Creed. This creed is the first official doctrinal statement of the Church and is the most ecumenical of all the creeds, being used by Roman Catholic, Eastern Orthodox, and many Protestant Christians alike. It was originally written by a gathering of bishops in the city of Nicea (in Turkey) in 325, and was later reaffirmed and revised in a similar meeting held in Constantinople in the year 381. The pressing question of the day was whether the divine in Jesus was the same eternal divinity present in God the creator. Most simply stated: Was Jesus God or a lesser, created being? The bishops at Nicea affirmed that Jesus was *homoousios* (of the same substance) with the Father; his divine nature was the same as God's divine nature. Many phrases were used to underscore this shared nature: God from God, light from light, true God from true God, begotten not made. As UCC theologian Lee Barrett says, "in Jesus Christ we are confronted with the very godness of God." The bishops at Constantinople extended this affirmation of divinity to the Holy Spirit.

The Definition of Chalcedon. Once it had been decided that Jesus' divinity was the same as God the Creator's, the most pressing question became, "How, then, are the divine and the human related in Jesus?" Did the divine nature take the place of a human soul? Did the human and divine natures merge into something new? Was Jesus really two persons in one body? Bishops gathered at Chalcedon in 451 to address these questions. In the end, they made two important affirmations. First, Jesus has two natures. His divine nature is the same as God's; his human nature is the same as ours, but without sin. Second, Jesus is just one person. The bishops did not explain how this works; on a fundamental level, the incarnation of God in human nature remains a mystery.

While these three statements set forth the basic affirmations of the church regarding the "person" of Christ (who he was and is), subsequent creeds, catechisms, and confessions have sought to explain, apply, and elaborate on the "work" of Christ (what Christ has done and continues to do for us). During the Reformation era (1500-1650), when Protestantism was first defined, a number of new creeds and confessions were written to help codify what these new Christian groups believed. Five of these documents have been especially significant for the traditions of the United Church of Christ.

Luther's Small Catechism. This catechism was written by Martin Luther in 1529 to teach the Christian faith to uneducated laity and children. He wanted all Christians to be doctrinally literate and especially to know that God was at work in Jesus Christ, who had been born, died and raised for their benefit. Salvation is God's gift, fully accomplished in Jesus Christ, and personally appropriated by the believer through God's own gift of faith. The catechism was brought to North America by German immigrants and became one of the texts providing an "authoritative interpretation" of scripture for the Evangelical and Reformed Church.

The Augsburg Confession. This confession too was authoritative for the Evangelical and Reformed Church and was especially prized in the German

Reformed tradition. It had been prepared by Luther's colleague, Philip Melanchthon, in 1530 as part of an attempt to reunite Protestant and Roman Catholic Christians. It stresses the shared beliefs of both groups, including ancient affirmations about who Jesus is. But it also strongly affirms justification by grace alone through faith alone which was a continuing point of disagreement between Protestants and Catholics.

The Heidelberg Catechism. This text also has roots in Germany and, after its composition in 1563, it became the chief statement of doctrine for the Reformed churches of Germany, the Netherlands and Hungary. It has come into the UCC through the Evangelical and Reformed Church. Originally designed to be acceptable to both Lutheran and Reformed Christians, it stresses God's redemptive activity in Christ. The Heidelberg Catechism has a personal, existential orientation, stressing hope and confidence. It also affirms God's sovereignty over the world and Christians' call to service.

The Westminster Confession. This substantial text was written in England in the mid-seventeenth century and has been the most important historical confession of faith for British and American Christians of the Reformed tradition. It was adopted by the Congregational Synod of the Massachusetts Bay Colony in 1648, with a few modifications relating to church organization and governance. The Connecticut Congregational churches also adopted it at the Synod of Saybrooke in 1708. Through this Congregational lineage it has become part of the theological heritage of the United Church of Christ. This confession seeks to bring all areas of life under the authority of God and the guidance of the Bible. Hence its treatment of Christ stresses the redemptive work of the Triune God, and it encourages political work in the world under God's sovereignty.

The Evangelical Catechism. This is the most modern of the historical texts we will be using. It was produced in the United States in the mid-nineteenth century to serve the churches of the German Evangelical Church Association of the West, later to become the Evangelical Synod of North America. Modeled on the Evangelical Church of the Prussian Union, founded in Germany to unite Reformed and Lutheran Christians, this group of churches sought to be ecumenical in spirit while cultivating heartfelt piety and vigorous discipleship. The catechism was written in 1847, revised in 1867, and translated from German into English in 1889. The version we will be using was authorized in 1929. It combines themes from Luther's Small Catechism and the Heidelberg Catechism. While affirming the ancient affirmations about Christ, it stresses how the drama of Christ's self-sacrificial love should encourage both gratitude in our hearts and concern for suffering humanity.

The Evangelical and Reformed traditions have brought more of these catechisms and confessions into our UCC heritage than the Congregational tradition. But, our Congregational forebears were not at all opposed to the use of such documents. In fact, many individual congregations in New England and elsewhere developed their own confessions of faith (often called "covenants") for use in worship and instruction. Many of these local statements were based on the Westminster Confession. In the UCC today, some churches recite a creed or confession of faith as part of their regular Sunday worship; others do not. Either way, we all have much to learn from these important documents that are part of our denominational heritage.

Other Resources for Reflection on Christ

In addition to the creeds described above, and in addition to various passages of scripture, this study guide also directs attention to two other resources for reflecting on who Christ was and is: (1) the words used in worship liturgies and (2) the texts of the songs and hymns that we sing. In a sense, these liturgical and musical resources represent our own present-day creeds in formation. They reflect beliefs about Christ that we hold dear in the age in which we live. Here are just a few examples of what we say and sing about Jesus.

Resources from Our Liturgies—taken from the *UCC Book of Worship* (1986):

> **Word & Sacrament I, Sentence of Adoration F, p. 36.** Jesus came to preach good news to the poor, to proclaim release to the captives and recovery of sight to the blind, to liberate those who are oppressed, and to proclaim the year of God's favor.

> **Word & Sacrament I, Communion Prayer B, pp. 45-46.** Above all, we give you thanks for the gift of Jesus, our only Savior, who is the way, the truth, and the life. In the fullness of time you came to us and received our nature in the person of Jesus, who, in obedience to you, by suffering on the cross, and being raised from

the dead, delivered us from the way of sin and death. We praise you that Jesus now reigns with you in glory and ever lives to pray for us.

Service of the Word I, Gloria B, p. 103. Lord Jesus Christ, God's only begotten one, Lord God, Lamb of God, you take away the sin of the world: have mercy on us; you are seated at the right hand of Majesty: receive our prayer. For you alone are the Messiah, you alone are the Lord, you alone are the Most High, Jesus Christ, with the Holy Spirit, in the glory of the triune God.

Resources from the Songs We Sing—taken from the *New Century Hymnal*. (We provide only selected phrases here and in the subsequent chapters. Why not pull out the hymnal and sing the whole song?)

#414, Incarnate God, Immortal Love. Incarnate God, immortal Love, whom we, that have not seen your face, by faith, and faith alone, embrace ... you gave us life ... We trust we were not made to die ... In you meet human and divine, the highest, holiest union known.

#507, Jesus—The Very Thought to Me. Jesus—the very thought to me with sweetness fills my breast; But sweeter far your face to see, and in your presence rest ... Savior of humankind. O hope of every contrite heart, O joy of all the meek ... Jesus, our joy, our greatest bliss, and you our prize will be; Our glory here and now is this, and through eternity.

#257, Alleluia! Gracious Jesus! Alleluia! Gracious Jesus! Yours the scepter, yours the throne! ... Yours the triumph, yours the victory alone! ... Jesus, out of every nation you've redeemed us by your blood ... You are near us ... shall our hearts forget your promise, "I am with you evermore." ... Here the sinful flee to you from day to day. Intercessor, friend of sinners, earth's Redeemer ... Christ eternal, nothing can disrupt your reign ... Born of Mary, heaven and earth are your domain. Human life you fully entered, tending those we count the least, serving both as Priest and Victim in the eucharistic feast.

In addition to these relatively formal resources for reflecting on the meaning of Jesus, we would also encourage every group that uses this book to allow time for those involved in the conversation to share their own more personal encounters with Christ. Some Christians, though certainly not all, have had profound, immediate experiences of Christ that have been deeply meaningful to them. Testifying about those experiences can be enriching for all. Christ is not only a figure from the past; he is alive and active in the world today and our own present-day experiences bear witness to that fact.

Questions for Discussion

- What kinds of situations prompt you to think about Jesus?

- How do you picture Jesus? What images come to mind?

- Where does your understanding of Jesus come from?

- Which, if any, of the creeds and confessions of the UCC does your congregation use?

- Which of the following words most closely describe Jesus' relationship with you: savior from sin, friend, guide, teacher, moral model, God, judge, source of power, victor over death, historical person? What other descriptions would you add?

- Do you think American Christians as a whole emphasize Jesus too much, not enough, or just about right? What about the UCC? What about your own congregation?

- What one or two things do you believe most strongly about who Jesus is, what he did, and how his followers should live today?

Prayer

Leader: Gracious God, we give you thanks for Jesus Christ, through whom all things came into being and who is present with us today through the Holy Spirit

People: We acknowledge your gift of Christ, who came that we might know of your love for all people, a love more wonderful than our imaginations can conceive.

Leader: Open our ears so that we may hear the voices of those who have gone before us.

People: Open our eyes also, that we may see our companions on the journey of faith and might glimpse the future that you desire to lay before us.

ALL: Grant us understanding and insight as we enter into this study, and be our guide. We pray in Jesus' name. Amen.

Chapter 2

Christ as God:
"You, God, Have Come to Us"

In Jesus Christ, the man of Nazareth,
our crucified and risen Savior,
you have come to us and shared our common lot,
conquering sin and death and reconciling
the world to yourself.

When speaking of Jesus Christ, the statements of faith that constitute our United Church of Christ heritage all begin by confessing that Jesus Christ was God come to earth. Jesus was not merely a good person, not merely a Spirit-filled person, and not merely a prophet; rather Jesus was God. The Nicene Creed affirms this with vigor and repetition: Christ was "God from God, Light from Light, true God from true God." Our creeds and confessions tell us many other things about Christ, but at the heart of the Christian claim is this: God has come to us in Jesus Christ.

As the Bible presents it, God's coming to us in Jesus is the culmination of a long series of divine actions through which humankind has slowly come to understand God better. The New Testament book of Hebrews begins, "Long ago God spoke to our ancestors in many and various ways by the prophets, but in these last days he has spoken to us by a Son." God has always spoken to humankind and God is still speaking today, but Jesus is the fullest and most complete revelation of God we will ever have.

Christians actually believe more than that—Jesus is not merely a revelation of God, Jesus *is* God. The medium is the message. Jesus is the sole God of the universe appearing in human form. Embodied in Christ, God's self-revelation was not a matter of mere words or ideas, but of flesh and blood. The first chapter of the Gospel of John says that God came "and lived among us, and we have seen his glory ... full of grace and truth."

This means that when we think about who God is, we ought first to think about God as Jesus, for Jesus is the human face of God. Therefore God is not, first of all, the most powerful force in the universe. Nor is God, first of all, the cosmic ruler who will someday judge our lives. Nor is God, first of all, the underlying sense of mystery that envelops our lives. God is all of those things, but, first of all, God is like Jesus. Jesus reveals God's personality, and the God Jesus reveals is compassionate, caring, embracing, forgiving, demanding, and understanding all at the same time.

God's deepest desire, fully displayed in the life of Jesus, is to live with us in a way that heals our wounded spirits and empowers us for moral goodness and extravagant love. The deep truth about God's self-revelation in Jesus Christ is that God is personal and seeks an intimate relationship with us that will restore our lives and make us capable of loving God and our neighbors.

The confession that God "comes to us" also reminds us that we cannot draw near to God by ourselves. When we encounter God, it is because God has initiated that encounter. God comes to us so that we, in turn, can approach God. There is no doubt that God's encounter with us involves our response. God comes to us seeking to be received and desiring that we will open our lives to the healing and

31

strengthening relationship God offers us. The manger scenes we display at Christmas perfectly illustrate the humble way in which the awesome God of the universe comes to us, not with overwhelming power, but with the gentleness of an infant, calling forth our own response of faith, love, and service.

In all of this, however, we should never forget that it is truly God who has come among us in Jesus. The babe in the manger is the creator of the world, the restorer of righteousness, and the reconciler of humanity with God. The Gospel of Luke says that Jesus cast out demons "by the finger of God" and goes on to say that he had power to defeat all the forces of evil that deform the world (Luke 11:20-22). The God who came to us in Christ is gentle and strong, loving and righteous, compassionate and just.

Questions for Discussion

- What is your picture of God when you pray?

- What personality characteristics do you associate with God?

- Do you normally think of Jesus as God?

What the Bible Says

(John 1:1-2, 18) In the beginning was the Word, and the Word was with God, and the Word was God. He was in the beginning with God. . . . No one has ever seen God. It is God the only Son, who is close to the Father's heart, who has made him known.

(John 16:28) I came from the Father and have come into the world.

(Matthew 1:20-23) "Joseph, son of David, do not be afraid to take Mary as your wife, for the child conceived in her is from the Holy Spirit. She will bear a son, and you are to name him Jesus, for he will save his people from their sins." All this took place to fulfill what had been spoken by the Lord through the prophet: "Look, the virgin shall conceive and bear a son, and they shall name him Emmanuel," which means, "God is with us."

(Colossians 1:19-20) For in him all the fullness of God was pleased to dwell, and through him to reconcile to himself all things, whether on earth or in heaven, making peace by the blood of his cross.

What Our Creeds Say

(Apostles' Creed) I believe in ... God's only Son, our Lord.

(Nicene Creed) We believe in one Lord, Jesus Christ, the only Son of God, eternally begotten of the Father, God from God, Light from Light, true God from true God, begotten not made, of one Being with the Father ... For us and for our salvation, he came down from heaven.

(Definition of Chalcedon) Our Lord Jesus Christ ... complete in Godhead ... truly God ... of one substance with the Father as regards his Godhead.

(Luther's Small Catechism II.ii) Jesus Christ, true God, begotten of the Father from eternity ... is my Lord.

(Heidelberg Catechism) Q. 35 What is the meaning of: "Conceived by the Holy Spirit, born of the Virgin Mary"?
A. That the eternal Son of God, who is and remains true and eternal God, took upon himself our true manhood from the flesh and blood of the Virgin Mary through the action of the Holy Spirit.
Q. 47 Then, is not Christ with us unto the end of the world, as he has promised us?
A. Christ is true man and true God.... in his divinity, majesty, grace, and Spirit, he is never absent from us.

(Westminster Confession VIII.ii) The Son of God, the second person in the Trinity, being very and eternal God, of one substance, and equal with the Father.

(Evangelical Catechism) Q. 60 Who is Jesus Christ?
A. Jesus Christ is true God and true man in one person, my savior, redeemer and Lord.
Q. 61 How does the Bible testify that Jesus Christ is true God?
A. In the Bible Jesus Christ is called God; furthermore, the Bible testifies to his divine nature and works, and demands divine honors for him.

What Our Liturgies Say—from the *UCC Book of Worship* (1986):

(Word and Sacrament I, Gloria A, p. 39) Lord Jesus Christ, God's only begotten one, Lord God, Lamb of God.

(Word and Sacrament I, Preface B, p. 45) In the fullness of time you came to us and received our nature in the person of Jesus.

(Word and Sacrament II, Preface B, p. 69) We thank you ... especially for Jesus Christ, whom you have sent from your own being as our Savior.

(Great Vigil of Easter, Collect after the First Lesson, p. 235) Almighty God ... grant that we may share the divine life of the one who came to share our humanity: Jesus Christ our Redeemer.

(Thanksgiving for One Who Has Died, Prayer at the death of a child, p. 378) Gentle God, born an infant in Jesus Christ in the family of Joseph and Mary.

(Advent, General Prayer, p. 479) Come to us in Christ, and show us the way to true life.

(Christmas, Call to Worship, p. 480) Jesus is our Emmanuel—God With Us—come to gather our tears and laughter, our work and play into God's love.

(Christmastide, Greeting, p. 483) God has been made known in Christ, the image of the invisible God, the firstborn of all creation.

(Epiphany, Confession, p. 488) Loving God, you have come to us in Jesus.

What Our Songs Say—from the *New Century Hymnal*:

(#135, O Come, All You Faithful) Come and behold the ruler of all angels ... God of true God, Light of true Light, born of the Virgin's womb in human form; Truly our God, begotten, not created.

(#162, In a Lowly Manger Born) In a lowly manger born ... this is God, the Human One! ... Came to earth for you and me, gave up life upon the tree; There we saw God's love revealed ... Our salvation now has come, gift of God, the Human One!

(#280, O Trinity, Your Face We See) O Trinity, your face we see through Christ in full humanity; For flesh has held divinity, that we might share your mystery.

(#414, Incarnate God, Immortal Love) Incarnate God, immortal Love ... In you meet human and divine, the highest, holiest union known.

Themes for Reflection

The Personal Trinity: The personal character of God—God being a "you" who comes to "us"—is one of the reasons Christians have traditionally believed that God is a Trinity composed of the Father and the Son and the Holy Spirit. God is relational. The three persons of the Trinity love each other in a way that is eternal and indissoluble, but does not eliminate the differences between them. The fullness of what that means is a mystery we will never understand, but it communicates very clearly that God is not an isolated or self-contained being. Quite the contrary, the love that exists within the Trinity is a love that both holds the Father, Son, and Holy Spirit together *and* overflows beyond the Trinity engulfing us and all of creation. God loves us and in Christ, God displayed that love in the most personal manner possible. Through Jesus, God invites us into the eternal circle of dynamic love that has forever defined God's own character and personality.

How God Speaks to Us: Jesus is sometimes called the "Word" of God. In the first chapter of the Gospel of John, it says that God has spoken to us through the "Word who became flesh." While Jesus is God's unique Word, there are many other ways that God has spoken and still speaks to humankind. Most notably, we hear God's voice speaking to us through the pages of the Bible; indeed, the Bible is our primary witness to Jesus' identity. We also hear God's voice in the writing of devout authors or the impassioned speech of preachers. We hear God speaking through social movements that call us to pursue peace, justice, and reconciliation. We hear God's whisper of reassurance in the soft and calming voice of a friend. We also hear God in the beauty and wonder of nature. While God can speak to us in all these different ways, we need to exercise discernment. Not every social movement is from God. Not every word spoken by a friend is true. Not every interpretation of the Bible is valid. How do we know when and where God is speaking? The traditional Christian answer—the answer of the creeds—is that these varied voices and words must eventually be tested against the special Word of God who was Jesus. Jesus remains the standard by which we seek to discern God's voice in the world today.

Personal Faith Journey: God's coming to us in Jesus is intended to give us the power to reorient our lives to God. Some Christians speak of a person turning to God as a decision that takes place in a moment. Other Christians prefer to speak of our response to God as a lifelong journey of deepening faith, trust, and confidence. However it begins or proceeds, our relationship with God will include such spiritual practices as prayer, Scripture reading, worship, fellowship with other believers and service. Our personal relationship with Jesus flows through these ways of living, bringing us both closer to God and closer to others. The goal isn't simply to get to heaven as if it were a reward separable from Jesus; instead, the goal is to be moving ever deeper into the loving life of God revealed in Jesus.

37

Questions for Discussion

- Does thinking of God as Jesus change your vision of God? Does thinking of Jesus as God change your vision of Jesus?

- What is unique about the way God has spoken to us in Jesus? What do we know about God that we wouldn't know without Jesus?

- What does it mean to have a personal relationship with God through Christ?

- Have there been times in your life when you were particularly aware of God coming to you? How did you sense this?

- How does our celebration of Christmas emphasize that this was God's special coming into the world?

- How might you explain the "good news" that God has come to us in Jesus to a friend or neighbor or child?

Prayer

All our prayers begin with wonder, God, at the love you show us in Jesus Christ. When we consider that you would come to us as a baby and share the life we know, no response we can make is adequate. Yet, you receive us as we are, your children, the human sisters and brothers of a Savior who was as human as we are and as divine as you are. You came to us in Jesus and you come to us still, inviting our response, calling forth our own love and compassion. Your compassion for us gives us hope for our world. Your caring empowers us to care for one another. Increase our understanding of this invitation and bring us into alignment with your will for the world. God, hear our prayer and grant us your presence, in and through Jesus. Amen.

Chapter 3

Christ as a Person in History:
"The Man of Nazareth"

*In Jesus Christ, **the man of Nazareth**,
our crucified and risen Savior,
you have come to us and shared our common lot,
conquering sin and death and reconciling
the world to yourself.*

Christians believe that Jesus was divine, but Christians, from the very beginning, have also asserted that Jesus was truly human as well—and Jesus' full humanity is as amazing as his divinity. Jesus was not God masquerading as a human being. There was nothing fake about his human body or his human mind. Quite the contrary, Jesus fully experienced all the defining features of what it means to be human.

Jesus had a mother. He cried when he was an infant. He grew up one year at a time just like everyone else, and when he was an adolescent, he undoubtedly caused his parents anxiety. At the very least, we know that when he was 12 he wandered off by himself during a family visit to the city of Jerusalem, and his parents fretted about where he was and what might have happened to him. When they finally found him at the temple discussing religious questions with the elders (Luke 2:41-51), they were almost certainly relieved and irritated at the same time, as any other parent would be.

Like every other human being, Jesus got tired and hungry. He sweated in the heat of summer. He experienced joy and dread. He enjoyed being with his friends. He prayed for God's strength and guidance. He impressed some people and he irritated others. He paid taxes. And he died. In every essential way, Jesus was human.

Jesus was not just human in a generic sense, he was also human in a very specific way: he was a Jew living in Palestine during a time when that region was occupied and ruled by the Roman Empire. He was born when Augustus was Caesar and Quirinius was Governor of Syria. It was a time when Jews were downtrodden and many longed for the overthrow of the Romans. He was circumcised eight days after his birth as was and is Jewish custom. He worshiped God in the synagogue and Temple. He studied the Hebrew Scriptures and celebrated Passover and Yom Kippur. He was an observant Jew, born into God's ongoing work with the people of Israel.

Jesus was particularly attracted to the prophetic strand of Jewish faith. It is therefore not surprising that, when he heard of a charismatic prophet named John who was baptizing people in the Jordan River, he went out to meet him and was baptized himself. In keeping with the long prophetic traditions of Israel, which included the public denunciation of the nation's religious failures, Jesus saw his role, at least in part, as calling Israel back to its own religious ideals. Prophets sometimes "spoke" with words and sometimes they "spoke" with actions. When Jesus violently cleared the Temple of merchants and money-changers saying that it had become a den of robbers (Mark 11:15-17), he was doing both: acting and speaking as a Jewish prophet of God.

Not long after his baptism by John, Jesus became a traveling teacher, preacher, and healer himself. The focus of his message was the "kingdom of God." According to Jesus, the kingdom of God existed wherever life was lived as God truly intended it, and that message raised moral expectations dramatically. In the "Sermon on the Mount" (found in Matthew 5-7), Jesus explained what he meant. While the old law said retribution was limited to "an eye for an eye," Jesus said his followers should forgo retribution altogether. In place of the commandment not to kill, he claimed it was wrong, even passively, to hate another human being. Regarding the sin of coveting the possessions of others, he said not only should we be content with what we have, we should never worry at all about what we are going to eat or drink or wear.

The point of Jesus' preaching was not to criticize Judaism and its laws; in fact, even as he ushered in a new era in God's relationship with humanity, Jesus reaffirmed Judaism's own highest ideals. It is not surprising that when Jesus was asked which commandment was the greatest of all, he responded in much the same way that his contemporary Rabbi Hillel had responded. Jesus said the highest commandment was to love God with every dimension of our being and to love our neighbors in the same way we would like to be loved ourselves (Matthew 22:36-40). It was not just that Jesus taught these things; he also lived what he taught. Nowhere is this more evident than at the time of his death when he prayed, while hanging on the cross, that God would forgive his executioners (Luke 23:34).

Whatever Jesus means to us today, it has to connect back to this very particular person who walked the dusty roads of Palestine two thousand years ago. Knowing Christ today requires that we understand Jesus as the man of Nazareth. This aspect of Christ's identity is not developed with any great detail in the historic creeds and confessions of the church nor is it emphasized in most of the liturgical and musical resources we use. Yet we need to remember

Jesus' Jewish particularity and his prophetic calling if we want to have a full picture of who Jesus was and still is.

Questions for Discussion

- Is it part of your image of Jesus to picture him as Jewish?

- How familiar are you with Judaism today? Do you have any close Jewish friends?

- As you think about Jesus' life as told in the Gospels, how is his humanity made evident?

What the Bible Says

(Luke 2:22-24, 39-40) When the time came for their purification according to the law of Moses, they brought him up to Jerusalem to present him to the Lord (as it is written in the law of the Lord, "Every firstborn male shall be designated as holy to the Lord"), and they offered a sacrifice according to what is stated in the law of the Lord, "a pair of turtledoves or two young pigeons." . . . When they had finished everything required by the law of the Lord, they returned to Galilee, to their own town of Nazareth. The child grew and became strong, filled with wisdom; and the favor of God was upon him

(Matthew 4:23) Jesus went throughout Galilee, teaching in their synagogues and proclaiming the good news of the kingdom and curing every disease and every sickness among the people.

(Mark 3:1-5) Again he entered the synagogue, and a man was there who had a withered hand. They watched him to see whether he would cure him on the Sabbath, so that they might accuse him. And he said to the man who had the withered hand, "Come forward." Then he said to them, "Is it lawful to do good or to do harm on the Sabbath, to save life or to kill?" But they were silent. He looked around at them with anger; he was grieved at their hardness of heart and said to the man, "Stretch out your hand." He stretched it out, and his hand was restored.

(Luke 19:45-47a) Then he entered the temple and began to drive out those who were selling things there; and he said, "It is written, 'My house shall be called a house of prayer'; but you have made it a den of robbers." Every day he was teaching in the temple.

What Our Creeds Say

(Luther's Small Catechism II.ii) I believe that Jesus Christ, true God, begotten of the Father from eternity, and also true man, born of the Virgin Mary, is my Lord.

(Heidelberg Catechism) Q. 35 What is the meaning of: "Conceived by the Holy Spirit, born of the Virgin Mary"?
A. That the eternal Son of God, who is and remains true and eternal God, took upon himself our true manhood from the flesh and blood of the Virgin Mary through the action of the Holy Spirit, so that he might also be the true seed of David.
Q. 47 Then, is not Christ with us unto the end of the world as he promised us?

A. Christ is true man and true God. As a man he is no longer on earth.

What Our Liturgies Say—from the *UCC Book of Worship* (1986):

(Word and Sacrament I, Doxology A, p. 43) Praise Christ the Word in flesh born low.

(Word and Sacrament I, Preface A, pp. 45-46) Born of Mary, our sister in faith, Christ lived among us.

(Ash Wednesday, Sentence, p. 180) Jesus came to preach good news to the poor, to proclaim release to the captives and recovery of sight to the blind, to liberate those who are oppressed, and to proclaim the year of God's favor.

(Great Vigil of Easter, Blessing of Water, p. 240) In the fullness of time, you sent Jesus Christ who was nurtured in the water of Mary's womb. Jesus was baptized in the water of the Jordan, became living water to a woman at the Samaritan well.

What Our Songs Say—from the *New Century Hymnal*:

(#161, Amen, Amen) O see the little baby lying in a manger on Christmas morning. See Jesus in the temple talking to the elders ... See Jesus at the seashore preaching to the people, healing all the sick ones! See Jesus on the cross ... in bitter agony!

(#162, In a Lowly Manger Born) In a lowly manger born, humble life begun in scorn. In a workshop Jesus grew, worker's struggles knew. Knew the suffering of the weak, knew the longing of the meek, Knew the poor and suffering ones; this is God, the Human One. Visiting each outcast soul, bringing peace to make them whole, Giving selflessly in love, God's own love to prove.

(#169, What Ruler Wades through Murky Streams) What ruler wades through murky streams and bows beneath the wave, Ignoring how the world esteems the powerful and brave? … Christ gleams with water brown with clay from land the prophets trod.

Themes for Reflection
Jewish-Christian Relations: As a Jew, Jesus belonged to a group of people who had a special relationship with God, but who had experienced and have continued to experience a great deal of historical oppression and rejection—often at the hands of their Christian neighbors and fellow citizens. This should never be. Jesus' Jewishness stands as a blunt reminder to those of us who are Christians that we need to honor God's long-term relationship with this particular people. The God whose kingdom Jesus announced and the God to whom Jesus prayed is the God of Abraham and Sarah. Thus, Christians affirm continuity between the Old Testament and the New Testament, as well as continuity between God's activity in Judaism and Christianity. In many ways we are called to be Jews at heart, and anti-semitism should never be associated in any way with the faith we profess in Jesus of Nazareth.

The Kingdom of God: In the Gospels, Jesus often describes himself as "the Son of Man." This term was used in the Old Testament to refer to someone who had a particular role to play in bringing about God's purposes on earth. It was used especially in reference to the one who was expected to come as the Messiah, the future king who would rule God's people with justice and love, and who would deliver them from their enemies. Jesus applied this label to himself, using it to evoke hope in the people of Israel and to point to his own messianic role. Jesus also redefined what the term meant. The kingdom of God, which Jesus both preached and inaugurated as "the Son of Man" was a kingdom of new values and relationships, rather than an empire of "politics as usual." It was a kingdom of humility and forgiveness, rather than a kingdom of coercive power and might. Thus, it is through the example of Jesus' weakness, suffering, obedience, and service that we learn what it means to be part of God's kingdom.

A Message of Liberation: Jesus' Jewish identity placed him among the oppressed people of the Roman world, so it is not surprising that he was especially attuned to the needs of the poor and downtrodden. What is equally significant is that Jesus' core message was one of liberation from bondage of all kinds. In Luke's Gospel, Jesus bursts forth proclaiming, "The Spirit of the Lord is upon me, because he has anointed me to bring good news to the poor. He has sent me to proclaim release to the captives and recovery of sight to the blind, to let the oppressed go free, to proclaim the year of the Lord's favor" (Luke 4:18-19). In contrast to the social norms of his day, Jesus forgave sinners and pronounced blessings on those who were poor, meek, and hungry for righteousness. He spoke freely with women about matters of faith, and he used women as exemplars of faith when debating with other religious teachers. He offered rest for those with heavy bur dens, living water for the thirsty, and bread for those seeking eternal life. He warned those who were rich, full, happy, and content in their conventional religiosity that destruction was near at hand. Jesus also healed people from the oppression of illness. Lepers and others suffering from diseases that made them social outcasts sought Jesus out. He healed them and, in doing so, he restored them to fellowship with others. Everyone did not warmly receive Jesus' message of liberation. Some felt threatened and lashed out against Jesus. If we follow Jesus' liberating way of life, we too may be perceived as dangerous.

Questions for Discussion

- Jesus was a prophet as well as the embodiment of God. Remembering that in the Bible a prophet is one who speaks God's truth to the world and not just a predictor of the future, what do you think Jesus might say as a prophet to our world today? What would be the equivalent today of Jesus' clearing the Temple of merchants and money-changers?

- How should Christians and Jews relate to each other today? How similar or different are our religious ideas, values, and practices?

- Jesus often used parables to describe the kingdom of God, comparing it to a mustard seed that grows into a great bush, a pearl worth all that one has, and a net that catches many fish. (See Matthew 13.) How would you describe the kingdom of God to people today?

- How are the words and actions of Jesus a source of liberation for us today?

- Are there ways in which you find Jesus threatening? How might someone see your own commitments and way of life as threatening?

- What is the "good news" for us in remembering Jesus in the particular time, place, and culture in which he lived? How might you explain this to a friend, a neighbor, or a child?

Prayer

All things are possible with you, God. You have given us access to you in ways we could not have imagined by coming to us in the man of Nazareth, our brother Jesus, the Messiah. In Jesus our predecessors have found, and we continue to find, a teacher, a healer, and Savior. We thank you that in Jesus we find the help we need to transform our abstract ideal of love into living, breathing ministry and mission. Continue to fill us with your love, we pray, that we may learn to embody Jesus Christ even as he embodied you. All this we pray from our hearts. Amen.

Chapter 4

Jesus as Fully and Perfectly Human: "Shared Our Common Lot"

In Jesus Christ, the man of Nazareth,
our crucified and risen Savior,
you have come to us and *shared our common lot*,
conquering sin and death and reconciling
the world to yourself.

The UCC Statement of Faith says succinctly that Jesus "shared our common lot." In a certain sense, this is merely an amplified way of saying that Jesus was truly human. But it goes beyond that. The point is not simply that Jesus was fully human; it is that Jesus experienced the full range of what it means to be human, and because he has experienced the fullness of human experience, Jesus can be a model for how we ourselves are called to live.

Jesus knows what it means to be hungry. He knows what it means to be tired. He knows what it means to be disappointed, misunderstood, and mistreated. He has experienced pain, both physical and emotional. He has experienced the feeling of being forsaken by God. He has even tasted death. His reactions were fully human. Think of Jesus in Gethsemane, praying to be spared the cross; sweating drops of blood. This was not play-acting. This was a human being facing a torturous death, but Christ remained faithful to God despite the pain involved. Further, Christ understands what it is to be tempted to sin and to struggle mightily to resist those temptations. In this, too, he serves as our model.

Christ also understands the positive side of life. During his years on earth, Jesus welcomed the simple pleasures of life: the beauty of meadow flowers, the joy of children at play, the fellowship of eating with friends. He appreciated times of celebration and occasionally joined in, most notably at one wedding party where he turned so much water into wine that the guests had more than they could possibly drink (John 2:1-11). Jesus had many friends including John, Peter, James, Mary, Martha, Lazarus, Joanna, and Zacchaeus, and he deeply valued the time he spent with them. When one of them died, Jesus did the same thing any of us would do: he wept at the loss of a friend.

In his life on earth, Christ revealed human life as it was meant to be lived. While all of humanity is created in the image of God, Jesus showed us what that image looks like when it is not marred by sin, pride, and self-centeredness. Jesus lived his life in keeping with the great commandments, that is, living in perfect love for God and other people. This love moved him to compassion for others. More than most of us, Jesus went out of his way to connect with individuals that others shunned. At the same time, he also rebuked sinners and called hypocrites to account. The love Christ modeled is a love that speaks the truth as well as a love that comforts the afflicted.

By living such a life, Jesus became, as the apostle Paul says, a "second Adam" who passes on to humankind the gift of life in place of the burden of sin and guilt (Romans 5:12-18). As we share this life, Jesus becomes the model of how we too can live more fully in the image of God. Christ shared the finiteness of our common lot as human beings. He suffered the worst we can imagine. Christ also seeks to raise our common lot through his exemplary life and saving work.

Questions for Discussion

- What is our "common lot"?

- Do you think God can really understand what it means to be human? Is it necessary that God do so?

- If Jesus reveals what it means to be truly human, what does our true humanity look like? What is and what is not part of our essential human nature?

What the Bible Says

(Genesis 1:27) So God created humankind in his image, in the image of God he created them; male and female he created them.

(Luke 6:12) Now during those days he went out to the mountain to pray; and he spent the night in prayer to God.

(John 11:32-36) When Mary came where Jesus was and saw him, she knelt at this feet and said to him, "Lord, if you had been here, my brother would not have died." When Jesus saw her weeping, and the Jews who came with her also weeping, he was greatly disturbed in spirit and deeply moved. He said, "Where have you laid him?" They said to him, "Lord, come and see." Jesus began to weep. So the Jews said, "See how he loved him!"

(Luke 22:39-42) He came out and went, as was his custom, to the Mount of Olives; and the disciples followed him. When he reached the place, he said to them, "Pray that you may not come into the time of trial." Then he withdrew from them about a stone's throw, knelt down, and prayed, "Father, if you are willing, remove this cup from me; yet not my will but yours be done."

(Matthew 27:46) And about three o'clock Jesus cried with a loud voice, "Eli, Eli, lema sabachthani?" that is, "My God, my God, why have you forsaken me?"

(Hebrews 4:15) We have not a high priest who is unable to sympathize with our weaknesses, but one who in every respect has been tested as we are, yet without sin.

(Philippians 2:5-8) Let the same mind be in you that was in Christ Jesus, who, though he was in the form of God, did not regard equality with God as something to be exploited, but emptied himself, taking the form of a slave, being born in human likeness. And being found in human form, he humbled himself and become obedient to the point of death—even death on a cross.

What Our Creeds Say

(Definition of Chalcedon) Our Lord Jesus Christ ... complete in humanity ... truly human, consisting of a rational soul and body ... of one substance with us as regards his humanity; like us in all respects, apart from sin ... begotten ... of Mary the Virgin.

(Augsburg Confession III) It is also taught among us that God the Son became man, born of the Virgin Mary, and that the two natures, divine and human, are so inseparably united in one person that there is one Christ, true God and true man, who was born, suffered, was crucified, died, and was buried.

(Westminster Confession VIII.ii) The Son of God, the second person in the Trinity, being very and eternal God, of one substance, and equal with the Father, did, when the fullness of time was come, take upon him man's nature, with all the essential properties and common infirmities thereof, yet without sin: being conceived by the power of the Holy Ghost in the womb of the Virgin Mary, of her substance.

(Evangelical Catechism) Q. 62 How does the Bible testify that the Son of God became true man?
A. Jesus Christ was conceived by the Holy Spirit and born of the Virgin Mary; he thereby entered into human nature and became in all things as we are, yet without sin.
Q. 72 In which passage of Holy Scripture do we find the humiliation and exaltation of Christ briefly described?
A. We find the humiliation and exaltation of Christ briefly described in the passage Philippians 2:5-11.

What Our Liturgies Say—from the *UCC Book of Worship* (1986):

(Word and Sacrament I, Preface B, p. 45) In the fullness of time you came to us and received our nature in the person of Jesus, who, in obedience to you, by suffering on the cross, and being raised from the dead, delivered us from the way of sin and death.

(Brief Order for One Who Is Sick, Preface, p. 92) We thank you especially that in the fullness of time you sent Jesus, born of Mary, to live in our midst, to share in our suffering, and to accept the pain of death at the hand of those whom Jesus loved.

(Baptismal Prayer, p. 141) In the fullness of time, you sent Jesus Christ, who was nurtured in the water of Mary's womb.

(Order for Marriage, Introduction A, p. 327) God gives joy. Through that joy, wife and husband may share their new life with others as Jesus shared new wine at the wedding in Cana.

(Christmastide, Call to Worship, p. 483) God has come to us in Jesus the Christ, to reconcile and make new. God has entered our existence of joy and sorrow, taking on human likeness in Jesus, born of Mary.

(Christmas, Confession, p. 481) You are not distant from us in some faraway heaven; you have come close to us in a child born of simple parents and cradled in a borrowed bed of straw.

What Our Songs Say—from the *New Century Hymnal*:

(#111, O Loving Founder of the Stars) Who grieving at the cry of pain—the anguish of our dying race ... O Christ, who braved earth's deepest pain.

(#498, Jesu, Jesu, Fill Us with Your Love) Knelt at the feet of his friends, silently washing their feet, Jesu, you acted as servant to them ... Loving puts us on our knees, showing our faith by our deeds, serving the neighbors we have from you.

(#209, O Love, How Vast, How Flowing Free) That God a human form should take, and mortal be for mortals' sake. Not as an angel visiting ... But born in flesh God chose to be, robed in our own humanity ... For us was tempted by the wrong, For us the pangs of hunger knew ... For us was beaten, whipped, and tried, and taken to be crucified.

(#506, What a Friend We Have in Jesus) What a friend we have in Jesus, all our sins and griefs to bear! ... Have we trials and temptations? Is there trouble any-where? We should never be discouraged; take it to our God in prayer! Can we find a friend so faithful, who will all our sorrows share? Jesus knows our every weakness; take it to our God in prayer!

Themes for Reflection
Christ Empathizes with Our Suffering: Jesus suffered, and because he did, we can approach our own suffering confident that God understands and walks beside us in our pain and weariness. Suffering is not an aberration, nor is it always God's way of punishing us for our sins. Instead, it is an ordinary part of life in the fallen world as we know it. We all suffer sometimes; no one is exempt. When others are suffering, Christians are called to weep with those who weep (Romans 12:15), and to pray for those who are too weighed down with despair to pray for themselves. When Christians themselves suffer, they lean on Christ and look to

the church (the body of Christ on earth) for aid and comfort. For most of us, it is easier to cope with "natural" suffering (such as a disease or an earthquake) than it is to deal with suffering caused by another human being—especially when that pain is caused intentionally. It was precisely that kind of intentional pain Jesus experienced on the cross. The Westminster Confession says Jesus "endured most grievous torments immediately in his soul, and most painful sufferings in his body." Because Christ understands even this worst kind of pain, we can be confident that God understands the full depth of our own suffering.

Christ Models Resisting Temptation: The Bible says Jesus was fully human and was thus capable of being tempted, just as all of us are. Yet, he resisted temptation, and in doing so he demonstrated that sin is not part of our essential human nature. Quite the contrary, sin defaces human nature and restricts rather than enhances our experience of life. What is sin? Sin is any action or attitude that undercuts the life God created us to live and enjoy, any action or attitude that undermines the way of life to which God calls us. The gospel story of Jesus' forty days of temptation and fasting in the desert (which is the basis for the forty days of Lent) provides a model for how we too can avoid sin. Jesus kept his attention focused on his God-given mission on earth, and he used scripture to help him keep his priorities straight. The temptations Jesus faced in the desert were extraordinary, involving the right and wrong use of his divine power, but Jesus was also tempted in many other more normal ways. Just like us, he was tempted to lie, tempted to hate, tempted to covet, and tempted to sexual immorality, but regardless of the circumstances Jesus never gave in to sin. Thus the Westminster Confession describes Jesus as taking "upon him man's nature, with all the essential properties and common infirmities thereof, yet without sin." It further elaborates that Jesus "being holy, harmless, undefiled, and full of grace and truth" perfectly fulfilled God's law. We need God's help to resist temptation, but God also knows that some temptations are almost impossible for us to resist. That is why Jesus taught his followers (in the Lord's Prayer) to pray to be delivered from temptation. Jesus understands our moral frailty and offers us his strength in need.

Christ Models Humble Service: Beyond resisting temptation, Christ also charted a new path of righteousness that we can follow—a path of righteousness that involves serving others rather than worrying about our own goodness. Jesus' whole life was one of humble service. The second chapter of the Letter to the Philippians (verses 6-11) contains an ancient Christian hymn that sets the stage, showing how humility made the incarnation possible. It praises Christ for "emptying himself" and taking on human form to show us how to live. When Jesus washed the feet of his disciples at the Last Supper, he sought to communicate this same theme. His message was that just as he had humbled himself to serve humankind, his followers were to humble themselves in service to others. Thus no task should ever be seen as "beneath us" if we are true followers of Christ.

Questions for Discussion

- Where in the life of Jesus do you see Jesus' humanity most clearly?

- When in the liturgical year is Jesus' humanity especially celebrated?

- Can Jesus be "fully human" and still be without sin? What does this tell us about ourselves?

- Some Christians wear clothing or jewelry with the letters "WWJD" meaning "What Would Jesus Do?" How and to what extent is Jesus a model for how we ought to live? In what situations do you look to Jesus as an example?

- How does Christ help us deal with suffering?

- How does Christ help us deal with temptation?

- How does Christ enable us to serve others with love and humility?

- How is knowing that Jesus was fully human "good news" for us? How might you explain that to a friend, a neighbor, or a child?

Prayer

Dear God, we confess that we are not everything you call us to be. Our lives are full of hopes and disappointments, but in Jesus, you have told us that you are always with us. When we are hungry and tired, remind us of your presence and your strength, always available to us. When we are tempted to follow our own ways, remind us that we are not our own, but belong to you. Lift the veil of our fears, so that we may build relationships characterized by forgiveness and healing. Teach us to resist the temptation to follow the ways of the world, and to embrace the path of new life you set before us. Move us into the joy of humble service. Hear our prayer, O God. Amen.

Chapter 5

Christ as Savior: "Crucified Savior, Reconciling the World to Yourself"

In Jesus Christ, the man of Nazareth,
our crucified and risen *Savior,*
you have come to us and shared our common lot,
conquering sin and death and
reconciling the world to yourself.

The purpose of the incarnation (God coming to us in Jesus) reaches a climax with the crucifixion. The message of Christianity is that somehow Christ's death on the cross—a death that he could have avoided—made it possible for us to be reconciled or put right with God. Christ's death opened a way for us to be at home in God's holy presence. In fact, Christ's death somehow reconciles the whole world to God. Christians have never claimed to fully understand how the death of Jesus makes this possible or why it had to take place in this way. Undoubtedly a full understanding of this remarkable event will remain beyond our reach until we see God face to face.

Crucifixion was a public spectacle. Its purpose was to humiliate the person being executed, to strike fear in the heart of anyone who shared the same values or actions as the one being killed, and to provide a grisly form of entertainment for the masses. Nailing troublemakers to a cross was part of the Roman Empire's iron-fisted way of keeping order, and it was reserved for criminals and political dissidents. There was nothing glorious about it. By design, crucifixion was a mean and painful form of execution, the worst way to die.

Why did Christ have to endure such a death? In part, the crucifixion completed Christ's full identification with the human experience, including life's most bitter possibilities. Something more was going on as well. In his death, Christ also took upon himself the entire burden of humanity's sin and, in so doing, Christ made it possible for us to be restored to full fellowship with God.

We defined sin earlier (p. 58) as any action or attitude that undermines the way of life for which God created us and to which God calls us, but sin involves more. Sin (in the singular) represents a deep flaw in our underlying character, and we commit sins (those many different actions or attitudes that contradict God's will) only because sin is already part of our character. Sin represents our general rebellion against God and against God's vision of how people should live. Sin is our attempt to claim that we can be our own "god"— deciding for ourselves what is right and wrong—rather than judging our wants and desires in the light of God's scale of values. Sin is a problem deeply rooted in the core of our motivations. This character flaw is much harder to deal with than any specific acts of sin. Part of becoming aware of the sin that exists within us as people is to discover that we are, in some very real sense, captive to sin's power and are unable to escape its grip through our own strength and determination. We need help from outside ourselves.

It is in response to this deeper problem of sin that Jesus' crucifixion comes into play, reconciling us to God—albeit in ways that are difficult, if not impossible, to put adequately into words. The Bible uses many different images and metaphors to explain what Christ's death means for us.

In one image, the list of our wrongdoings is nailed to the cross (Colossians 2:14). Our sins are no longer held against us. In another image, Christ is portrayed as our substitute who accepts the penalty for our sin in his suffering and death. Christians often use the poetic language of the book of Isaiah to communicate this aspect of the cross:

> . . . he was wounded for our transgressions,
> crushed for our iniquities;
> upon him was the punishment that made us whole,
> and by his bruises we are healed" (Isaiah 53:5).

The Old Testament practice of sacrifice provides the background for this passage, and the New Testament book of Hebrews explains how Christ served as both the sacrifice offered in our place and the high priest who offered that sacrifice on our behalf (Hebrews 9:11-15).

In his trial and crucifixion, Jesus experienced the hate, injustice, alienation, cruelty, hurt, rejection, and separation that sin imposes on all those held in its grasp even though his own heart was free of any hint of rebellion against God. Christ voluntarily entered into our condition to "save" or "redeem" us, and this provides us with a third image: Christ as our redeemer who "buys us back" as if from a slave market or a prison camp (1 Corinthians 6:20). In this understanding, Christ's life became the payment that frees us from bondage.

Yet another way of understanding the crucifixion focuses on the manner in which Christ responded to those involved in the process of his execution. What is central here is not so much suffering or payment for sin, but unconditional forgiveness. The innocent Christ is arrested, tortured, and finally nailed to the cross. Even at the point of death, however, Jesus does not succumb to evil, but instead prays that his enemies will be forgiven (Luke 23:34). He absorbs our evil and offers us goodness in its place. If Jesus can forgive his own murderers, can anything else be beyond God's forgiveness?

As varied as they are, the common thread that runs through all of these different explanations of the crucifixion is that Christ does for us what we cannot do for ourselves. We cannot undo the harm we have done to others. We cannot forgive ourselves. We cannot banish evil from the world or even from our own hearts. Nor can we make things right between God and ourselves. We need help and Christians find the reconciling help they need in Christ and in the cross.

While the primary emphasis of the Christian message is on the reconciliation of believers with God and one another, it seems as if the reconciling work of Christ will ultimately extend to all of creation. In his Letter to the Romans, Paul asserts that the entire universe is "groaning in labor pains" awaiting the day when "the creation itself will be set free from its bondage to decay and will obtain the freedom of the glory of the children of God" (8:19-23). The Letter to the Colossians also says that everything in heaven and on earth is somehow included in the scope of Christ's reconciliation. Our individual redemption is part of something much larger than ourselves: in Christ, God is restoring the moral order and beauty that the entire creation was always meant to possess.

Questions for Discussion

- When we pause in worship to confess our sins, what kinds of actions and attitudes do you examine in your own life? Do you ever feel like a rebel against God?

- What is your gut reaction to Jesus' death? How do you think you would have reacted if you were present at the crucifixion?

- What images or metaphors for what happened on the cross speak most profoundly to you?

What the Bible Says

(Romans 5:8-11) But God proves his love for us in that while we still were sinners Christ died for us. Much more surely then, now that we have been justified by his blood, will we be saved through him from the wrath of God. For if while we were enemies, we were reconciled to God through the death of his Son, much more surely, having been reconciled, will we be saved by his life. But more than that, we even boast in God through our Lord Jesus Christ, through whom we have now received reconciliation.

(2 Corinthians 5:18-21) All this is from God, who reconciled us to himself through Christ, and has given us the ministry of reconciliation; that is, in Christ God was reconciling the world to himself, not counting their trespasses against them, and entrusting the message of reconciliation to us. So we are ambassadors for Christ, since God is making his appeal through us; we entreat you on behalf of Christ, be reconciled to God. For our sake he made him to be sin who knew no sin, so that in him we might become the righteousness of God.

(Colossians 1:19-20) In him all the fullness of God was pleased to dwell, and through him God was pleased to reconcile to himself all things, whether on earth or in heaven, by making peace through the blood of his cross.

(Colossians 2:13-14) And when you were dead in trespasses … God made you alive together with him, when he forgave us all our trespasses, erasing the record that stood against us with its legal demands. He set this aside, nailing it to the cross.

(Isaiah 53:12) He poured out himself to death, and was numbered with the transgressors; yet he bore the sin of many, and made intercession for the transgressors.

(John 15:12-13) This is my commandment, that you love one another as I have loved you. No one has greater love than this, to lay down one's life for one's friends.

(1 Peter 2:24) He himself bore our sins in his body on the cross, so that, free from sins, we might live for righteousness; by his wounds you have been healed.

What Our Creeds Say

(Luther's Small Catechism II.ii) I believe that Jesus Christ, true God, begotten of the Father from eternity, and also true man, born of the virgin Mary, is my Lord, who has redeemed me, a lost and condemned creature, delivered me and freed me from all sins, from death, and from the power of evil, not with silver and gold but with his holy and precious blood and with his innocent sufferings and death, in order that I may be his, live under him in his kingdom, and serve him in everlasting righteousness, innocence, and blessedness.

(Heidelberg Catechism) Q. 29 Why is the Son of God called Jesus, which means Savior?

A. Because he saves us from our sins and because salvation is to be sought or found in no other.

Q. 37 What do you understand by the word "suffered"?

A. That throughout his life on earth, but especially at the end of it, he bore in body and soul the wrath of God against the sin of the whole human race, so that by his suffering, as the only expiatory sacrifice, he might redeem our body and soul from everlasting damnation, and might obtain for us God's grace, righteousness, and eternal life.

(Westminster Confession VIII.v) The Lord Jesus, by his perfect obedience and sacrifice of himself, which he through the eternal Spirit once offered up unto God, hath fully satisfied the justice of his Father, and purchased not only reconciliation, but an everlasting inheritance in the kingdom of heaven, for all those whom the Father hath given unto him.

(Evangelical Catechism) Q. 60 Who is Jesus Christ?

A. Jesus Christ is ... my savior, redeemer and Lord.

Q. 63 How did Christ reveal himself as the savior before his death?

A. Christ revealed himself as the Savior before his death by his holy life, in which he perfectly fulfilled the Law of God; by his preaching the forgiveness of sin through faith in him; by his miracles, which are all works of life.

Q. 64 Whereby did Christ accomplish our redemption?

A. Christ accomplished our redemption by his suffering and death, in which he endured, in our stead, the wrath of God against sin, thereby redeeming us from sin, Satan, and death.

Q. 65 Why was the death of Christ necessary for our redemption?

A. The death of Christ was necessary for our redemption because we, lost sinners, could be redeemed neither by teaching nor by example, but only by the sacrifice of our Lord Jesus Christ in his suffering and death.

What Our Liturgies Say—from the *UCC Book of Worship* (1986):

(Word and Sacrament I, Preface B, p. 45) In the fullness of time you came to us and received our nature in the person of Jesus, who, in obedience to you, by suffering on the cross, and being raised from the dead, delivered us from the way of sin and death.

(Word and Sacrament I, Communion Prayer B, p. 48) We offer to you ourselves, giving you thanks for the perfect offering of the only one begotten by you, Jesus Christ our Savior.

(Baptism, Address B, pp. 135-136) Baptism is the sacrament through which we are united to Jesus Christ and given part in Christ's ministry of reconciliation. Baptism is the visible sign of an invisible event: the reconciliation of people to God. It shows the death of self and the rising to a life of obedience and praise.

(Lent, Invocation, p. 491) We gather to worship, O God, under the shadow of the cross, sign of human shame and divine wisdom. Like Jesus, we would follow faithfully in your way; like Jesus, we would live to you and die to you.

(Lent, General Prayer, p. 493) We thank you that Jesus walked the path of obedience all the way to the cross and that you raised Jesus up to draw us to yourself.

(Great Vigil of Easter, Easter Proclamation, p. 232) For Christ has ransomed us with the blood and for our salvation has paid you the cost of Adam and Eve's sin!

What Our Songs Say—from the *New Century Hymnal*:

(#218, Ah, Holy Jesus) For me, kind Jesus, was your incarnation, your mortal sorrow, and your life's oblation, Your death of anguish and your bitter passion, for my salvation.

(#220, Sing, My Tongue) God then chose the way: Chose the tree to bear the Savior ... Thus the plan of our salvation: God for all our sin would pay ... Born to fill this sacred moment, facing death with full intent, For the sacrifice of ages, to the cross the Lamb is sent.

(#226, O Sacred Head, Now Wounded) O sacred Head, now wounded, with grief and shame weighed down ... What you, dear Savior, suffered was all for sinners' gain; Mine, mine was the transgression, but yours the deadly pain.

(#229, Were You There?) Were you there when they crucified my Lord? O sometimes it causes me to tremble, tremble, tremble.... Were you there when they nailed him to the tree?

Themes for Reflection

Reconciliation Is Costly: As we consider the crucifixion, we come to understand that Christ's death can be viewed both as an action offered to God by Jesus and as an action offered by God to us. From either perspective, grace is costly. The reconciliation made possible by Christ's death involves pain and suffering of a kind we can know only in part. The analogy of a parent watching a beloved child being put to death communicates the intensity of what was involved. In the crucifixion God says to us: "I will go to the most painful ends to be with you." While salvation began with God's initiative and would have been impossible without that initiative, reconciliation is also costly for us. The German theologian Dietrich Bonhoeffer, executed during World War II for his resistance to the Nazi regime, said the call to follow Jesus is a call to die. In order to grip hold of the reconciliation God offers us, we must let go of our old sinful selves. In fact, we must "die to self"—a phrase intended to communicate the power sin has over us, and the difficulty we have giving sin up. Unless we put to death the habits and desires of sin, we can never experience true fellowship with God or others. Once again, it is important to remember that we cannot do this on our own. God helps us, but we still need to hear Jesus' words, "If any want to become my followers, let them deny themselves and take up their cross and follow me" (Matthew 16:24).

Repentance: Christ's crucifixion is the event that makes possible God's gracious forgiveness of our sin. We are forgiven by God and that forgiveness carries no strings. Yet, there are proper and improper ways of responding. The improper response is to make light of the seriousness of our sin and to act as if sinning or not sinning is of little consequence. Such an attitude demeans the cross. The proper attitude is to repent. In fact, the sixteenth-century Protestant

71

Reformer Martin Luther said in his famous *Ninety-five Theses* that the cross calls us to a life of continual repentance. To repent means to turn around, in particular, to turn away from sin and turn back to God. Repentance requires both self-examination and the acknowledgment of our sin and disobedience of God's law. For many centuries the church has set aside the time of Lent—the forty days before Easter—as a time for Christians to remind themselves of their continuing need for repentance. During this time period especially, we seek to renounce our sin and aimless ways of living as we simultaneously seek to become more deeply reconciled with God and those around us. While we experience repentance as hard work, it really is a gift from God. Through repentance God enables us to slowly let go of the desire to control our own lives and destinies and to understand our place in the gracious kingdom where God rules. Luther's *Small Catechism* says the goal of repentance is to "live under him in his kingdom, and serve him in everlasting righteousness."

Transformation: The saving work of God accomplished in Jesus Christ is not simply exterior work done to us— something that changes our formal status with God—it also changes us from the inside. As the human and divine were joined in Christ's own life, so God's own nature is dynamically grafted onto our nature in salvation. The Gospel of John says we are "born again" (John 3:3). When Jesus said he was the way, the truth, and the life (John 14:6), he meant that the deepest truth about salvation is personal and transformative. In Jesus we see both the model and the source of the God-filled existence God wants for all of us. Through the influence of the Holy Spirit, Christ transforms our sin-filled lives with his own sin-conquering life. The One who defeated sin and death on the cross frees us from sin's grip. This is why the Evangelical Catechism, in particular, speaks of the *necessity* of Christ's death. We need more than Christ's teaching to set us on the right path. We need more than Christ's good example to motivate us to action. We even need more than mere forgiveness to make us new creatures. What we need is the awe-inspiring power unleashed by Christ's death. It is that power, transferred to us by the Holy Spirit, that breaks our addiction to sin, strengthens our attraction to godliness, and grants us the genuine newness of life we seek.

Questions for Discussion

- How does Jesus' death enable us to be reconciled with God?

- Did Jesus have to die? Why?

- Have you ever experienced an especially powerful moment of reconciliation with God?

- In what ways do you sense a need for further reconciliation with God?

- How can the church help individuals and society be reconciled with God? What might it mean for "the world" to be reconciled to God? What might this mean for a nation and national politics? What might this mean for the natural world?

- What is the "good news" for us in the death of Jesus? How might you explain that "good news" to a friend, a neighbor, or child?

Prayer

Leader: In Christ our Savior, God came to earth to restore us to right relationship with God and one another.

People: God, we receive with joy the good news of your love and forgiveness.

Leader: No one way of explaining Christ's death is sufficient.

People: In every way, we acknowledge that Christ does what we cannot do for ourselves.

Leader: We cannot defeat evil by our own efforts. We cannot forgive ourselves.

People: But in Jesus Christ, O God, you have done all that is necessary. We will seek to live as your people, transformed for a future that only you can see.

Leader: People of God, release your old life and embrace the new.

ALL: O God of mercy, make us desire to be reconciled, new creations in our crucified and risen Savior. Amen.

Chapter 6

A New Life: "Risen Savior, Conquering Sin and Death"

In Jesus Christ, the man of Nazareth,
our crucified and *risen Savior*,
you have come to us and shared our common lot,
conquering sin and death and reconciling
the world to yourself.

Christians are "Easter people." Christians proclaim Jesus' resurrection from the dead and the new life that this makes available to believers. While Jesus' death on the cross put us right with God, Jesus' resurrection shows us that neither suffering nor death nor our own aimlessness and sin will have the last word. Christ is risen! The cross is now an empty cross and the tomb is now an empty tomb because Christ lives. As a consequence of Christ's resurrection, we have hope for the future. We also have access to God's power in a new way, helping us to overcome the sin, evil, and suffering that continue to haunt the world. Resurrection life—the life offered us by the living Christ who is still present in our midst—is at the center of active, vibrant Christian faith.

The church has affirmed, from its beginning, that through his death Jesus entered into combat with the powers of death and evil. The Apostles' Creed says Jesus "descended to the dead." In doing so, he invaded the home territory of all the oppressive spiritual forces that are aligned against God and God's will for the world. Once there, the Letter to the Colossians says, "he disarmed the rulers and authorities and made a public example of them, triumphing over them in [the cross]" (2:15). As the victor over these forces of sin and evil, Christ frees us from their grip.

Who or what are these hostile forces, these "tyrants," which have held humanity in bondage for so long? Different explanations have been offered. Some think of them as spiritual beings, others understand them as simply part of the chaotic dynamics of the universe. Still others believe they are symbols of the destructive addictions and compulsions that bedevil us as individuals and of the oppressive structures that deform society. However we conceive these forces, Christians believe that when Jesus rose again, they were decisively defeated. While we may still experience sin, evil, and death as negative realities, the power sustaining them has been broken and their lasting effects rendered merely temporary. This is because the power unleashed by Christ's resurrection is the power of God to heal the world and make all things right.

Indeed, Jesus' whole life on this earth was a battle against the deeply ingrained powers of sin, sickness, decay, and death in the world. His goal was liberation from all such bondage. For example, in the story of the Gerasene demoniac, Jesus casts out a "legion" of ills, restoring to wholeness a man whose life was out of control (Mark 5:1-20). People are not the only objects of Christ's liberating power; the natural world also participates in this new freedom as bread is multiplied and winds are calmed (Matthew 14:13-36; Romans 8:21).

Jesus' victory in his battle with evil and oppression becomes evident when God raises him from the dead—and that resurrection victory came as a surprise to almost everyone, including his own disciples. They had not known what to expect after Jesus was executed, nor did they actually see him rise. When they did encounter Jesus after the resurrection, they did not always recognize him because he was changed. The resurrected Christ walked, talked, and ate with his disciples. He invited them to touch him to see that he was real. Yet, he was also different. The resurrected Jesus appeared and disappeared in a way the pre-crucifixion Christ never did. He even passed through locked doors. (See John 20:11-29.) He was the same man of Nazareth they had known—they were convinced of that—but Christ's resurrected life also revealed the new creation that awaits us all.

As the disciples encountered this risen Christ, they were empowered for mission and given the charge to bear witness to Christ and preach forgiveness of sins in his name throughout the world. They were also empowered to live lives of love for God and neighbor. They did all of this looking forward to and longing for the day when their mortal bodies would put on immortality and they would live forever in the eternal kingdom of God's future. Christ's encounter with the disciples fueled their testimony, nurtured their compassion for others, and gave them hope for the future, despite the opposition they sometimes experienced.

Questions for Discussion

- What do you think really happened on Easter morning?

- Do you think that the resurrection of Christ is something that we should be able to fully understand and explain?

- How have you experienced the power of the resurrection in your own life?

(Matthew 8:1-3) When Jesus had come down from the mountain … there was a leper who came to him and knelt before him, saying, "Lord, if you choose, you can make me clean." … Immediately his leprosy was cleansed.

(Mark 2:9-12) "Which is easier, to say to the paralytic, 'Your sins are forgiven,' or to say, 'Stand up and take your mat and walk'? But so that you may know that the Son of Man has authority on earth to forgive sins"—[Jesus] said to the paralytic—"I say to you, stand up, take your mat and go to your home." And he stood up, and immediately took the mat and went out before all of them; so that they were all amazed and glorified God.

(1 Corinthians 15:17-23) If Christ has not been raised, your faith is futile and you are still in your sins. Then those also who have died in Christ have perished. If for this life only we have hoped in Christ, we are of all people most to be pitied. But in fact Christ has been raised from the dead, the first fruits of those who have died. For since death came through a human being, the resurrection of the dead has also come through a human being; for as all die in Adam, so all will be made alive in Christ. But each in his own order: Christ the first fruits, then at his coming those who belong to Christ.

(Acts 2:24) But God raised [Jesus of Nazareth] up, having freed him from death, because it was impossible for him to be held in its power.

(Romans 6:9-11) We know that Christ, being raised from the dead, will never die again; death no longer has dominion over him. The death he died, he died to sin, once for all; but the life he lives, he lives to God. So you also must consider yourselves dead to sin and alive to God in Christ Jesus.

(Colossians 2:15) He disarmed the rulers and authorities and made a public example of them, triumphing over them in [the cross].

(John 12:31-32) Now is the judgment of this world; now the ruler of this world will be driven out. And I, when I am lifted up from the earth, will draw all people to myself.

What Our Creeds Say

(Apostles' Creed) Jesus Christ suffered under ... Pontius Pilate, was crucified, died, and was buried; he descended to the dead. On the third day he rose again.

(Luther's Small Catechism II.ii) Jesus Christ ... who has redeemed me, a lost and condemned creature, delivered me and freed me from all sins, from death, and from the power of the devil ... is risen from the dead and lives and reigns to all eternity.

(Augsburg Confession III) Christ ... truly rose from the dead on the third day ... that he may bestow on [all who believe in him] life and every grace and blessing, and that he may protect and defend them against the devil and against sin.

(Heidelberg Catechism) Q. 45 What benefit do we receive from "the resurrection" of Christ?
A. First, by his resurrection he has overcome death that he might make us share in the righteousness which he has obtained for us through his death. Second, we too are now raised by his power to a new life. Third, the resurrection of Christ is a sure pledge to us of our blessed resurrection.

(Evangelical Catechism) Q. 60 Who is Jesus Christ?
A. Jesus Christ is ... my savior, redeemer and Lord.
Q. 68 What does it mean to us that Jesus Christ rose from the dead?
A. The resurrection of Jesus Christ proves that he is the Son of God; that he is our Redeemer, in whom we have newness of life; and that we also shall be raised from the dead.

What Our Liturgies Say—from the *UCC Book of Worship* (1986):

(Word and Sacrament I, Preface B, pp. 45-46) In the fullness of time you came to us and received our nature in the person of Jesus, who, in obedience to you, by suffering on the cross, and being raised from the dead, delivered us from the way of sin and death.

(Brief Order for One Who Is Sick, p. 92) We rejoice that in a perfect victory over the grave you raised Christ with power to become sovereign in your realm.

(Committal B, p. 387) ... believing that as you raised Jesus Christ from death, you will breathe life into us again so that we may live with you forever.

(Great Vigil of Easter, Easter Proclamation, p. 232) This is the night when Jesus Christ broke the chains of death and rose triumphant from the grave.

(Easter, General Prayer, p. 497) In the resurrection, you were victorious over sin, violence, and oppression.

(Eastertide, General Prayer, p. 500) We praise you, O God, that by the life, death and resurrection of Jesus Christ, you have delivered us from the power of death, making us alive to serve you.

What Our Songs Say—from the *New Century Hymnal*:

(#230, Come, You Faithful, Raise the Strain) Christ has burst from prison, And from three days' sleep in death as the sun has risen; All the winter of our sins, long and gray, is flying.

(#233, Christ the Lord Is Risen Today) Where, O death, is now your sting? ... Dying once, Christ lives to save ... Where your victory, O grave? ... Love's redeeming work is done ... Fought the fight, the battle won ... Death in vain forbids Christ rise ... God has opened paradise.

(#234, I'll Shout the Name of Christ Who Lives) I'll shout the name of Christ who lives ... that all might live; Christ broke death's power at Calvary, and now I know from sin I'm free.

(#242, The Strife Is O'er) The strife is o'er, the battle done, the victory of life is won; The song of triumph has begun ... The powers of death have done their worst, but Christ their legions has dispersed: Let shouts of holy joy outburst ... Christ, by your wounds on Calvary from death's dread sting your servants free, That we may live eternally.

Themes for Reflection

Our Resurrection: Scripture affirms that God raised Jesus from the dead and because of that, we can look for a similar resurrection at God's hand. This conviction has been asserted through the centuries in creeds, confessions, and catechisms. Human beings are not immortal. We are all subject to death. Any victory over death is God's doing and it is God's gift. The church has never taught that the soul by its very nature is eternal. Nor has it ever said resurrection is an expression of natural renewal like springtime. Resurrection is also different from merely being brought back to life as in a medical near-death experience. Our lives will be restored to us, and we will also fully become the new creatures we desire to be and Christ intends us to be. The good news of the resurrection is that God is both stronger than death and stronger than all the other forces in the universe that would keep us in bondage. Someday we will experience that resurrected life in its fullness, but we can also experience that life to some degree right now. This is, in fact, what the phrase "eternal life" means (John 3:16). The word translated as "eternal" indicates both "without end" and "of a higher quality." We can enjoy that higher quality of life today as we look forward with hope to never-ending life with God and all the saints.

Resurrection and the Breaking of Bread: In the New Testament it says that the disciples recognized the risen Christ when he ate a meal with them (see Luke 24:13-35). Luke tells us that while sitting at table with two disciples Jesus took bread and blessed it and then he broke it and gave it to them to eat. Jesus does the same for us today. Each time we participate in the Eucharistic celebration, we remember both Christ's death and Christ's resurrection. Moreover, it is not just bread we bring to the table in the communion service, we bring our entire lives to the table of Christ. There we ask Christ to bless us through the bread and the wine, feeding us with his body and blood, sharing his own resurrection life with us. We are changed by that encounter in the same way the disciples were changed by their interactions with the risen Christ, and our lives are transformed. By God's grace, sin is conquered, our aimlessness is given direction, and we are empowered to love God and serve others.

Already, But Not Yet: Although Christ has truly conquered sin and death, none of us will experience the fullness of that victory during our lives on earth. Christ's victory over the forces of sin and evil was decisive, but it is not yet complete. An analogy from nature helps explain our experience. We may be able to pick the first ripe tomato in July, but the many green tomatoes that remain will have to endure rainstorms, insect infestation, and the risk of disease before they ripen on the vine sometime in August or September. Something similar is going on in the world today. Ours is a time of waiting for the full harvest of which Jesus' resurrection was the "first fruit." Much of life is like this. The only way to win a game of soccer is to play the whole ninety minutes, even if the winning goal was scored five minutes into the game. When a symphony begins, the practiced ear knows what the final chord will be, even though there will be various developments and even discord along the way. A strep throat still hurts after the course of antibiotics has begun, but the defeat of the bacteria is assured. None of these analogies adequately explains the already-but-not-yet victory over evil and oppression we possess because of Christ's resurrection, but something similar is involved. Although we do not know all the details, we believe that the fullness of God's kingdom of love and righteousness is presaged in Christ's victory over death. Because of that, we can live confidently in the assurance of God's coming kingdom, working in many different ways to help make Christ's victory evident. In the same way that Jesus brought new life to people during his earthly ministry, we are called to do the same. As Jesus fed the hungry and forgave sinners, so should we. As Jesus fought evil, we too should join in the effort to make our world more just and peaceable and kind. As Jesus proclaimed the hope of a life that death could not conquer, so should we. In living this way, we will experience an ever-deeper awareness of the power and promise that is ours in and through Christ's resurrection.

Questions for Discussion

- Does Good Friday or Easter play a bigger role in your Christian faith? How are these events celebrated in worship?

- Jesus conquered his own death in the resurrection, but what does that mean for us? How is death conquered in our own lives?

- How did Jesus conquer sin? What does this mean? Is sin declining in the world or increasing?

- Do you struggle with sin in your own life? How can Jesus help you conquer sin? Can we ever live sinless lives?

- What sins or evils that hold people in bondage are we especially called to resist in the world around us?

What would victory over those sins look like? Can you think of people who have lived lives in the victory of the resurrection?

- How often do you think about dying? What are your thoughts and feelings about death and dying? To what degree is hope for your own resurrection a significant part of your personal faith?

- How might you explain the "good news" of the resurrection of Jesus to a friend, a neighbor, or a child?

Prayer

We are your Easter people, dear God. Like the women and men who first followed Jesus, we are afraid to recognize you. You and you alone are able to open our eyes. We encounter you in places where we don't expect to see you. We see the risen Christ in surprising ways. By these, our encounters with resurrection, we are empowered for mission, enabled to share the love of Christ, and engaged in the ministries of proclamation, justice, peace, and compassion that were given us by Jesus while he walked the earth. Help us to live in victory of the resurrection. In the peace of Christ, Amen.

Chapter 7

Jesus as Ruler and Giver of the Holy Spirit: "Our Lord"

In Jesus Christ, the man of Nazareth,
our crucified and risen *Lord*, [God]
has come to us ... He bestows upon us his Holy Spirit,
creating and renewing the church of Jesus Christ,
binding in covenant faithful people of
all ages, tongues, and races.

Following his resurrection, the book of Acts tells us that Christ spent forty days on earth with his disciples before he ascended into heaven to exercise his rule over all the earth. In the language of the creeds that form our UCC heritage, the ascension of Jesus is paired with the affirmation that Christ is now "sitting at the right hand of God," a metaphorical way of saying he has divine power and authority. Even though he has ascended to this lofty position, however, Jesus remains deeply and intimately concerned with us and our world and, through the work of the Holy Spirit, he comforts and empowers us.

The phrase "Jesus is Lord" has been a commonly repeated refrain throughout the centuries of Christian worship. The word "Lord" is also used in the 1959 version of the UCC Statement of Faith seen above. When Christians speak of Jesus as Lord, they mean two things. First, Jesus is identified with God as the rightful ruler of the world.

Second, Jesus, and Jesus alone, is presented as the ruler of the world, which implies that no other political, economic, social, or cultural ruler either deserves or has the right to claim our undivided allegiance.

In everyday usage, the word "lord" is a title for a man with rank and power like a king. In our democratic society, we tend to hear this with negative overtones: autocratic rule, patriarchy, racial discrimination, slavery, despotism, and elitism. Indeed, as we look at various "lords" in the course of history, we repeatedly see these difficulties. The lordship of Christ is different, however. Rather than "lording" his rule over us in a way that makes life more difficult, the lordship of Christ actually frees us to live life as it was meant to be lived. Christ's lordship reorients our lives by relativizing the power of other earthly lords. When faced with the power of the Roman authorities, the disciples said they served no lord but God alone (Acts 5:29). It is the lordship of Christ that allows us to confront all the oppressive lords of this earth, whether they be "lords" of political power or racial prejudice or gender oppression or economics or any other force that deforms human life as God intends it.

Thus, it is clear that Jesus' lordship has political ramifications. Human rulers often abuse their powers and need to be called to account. We should be careful, however, not to simply equate the freedom that comes with Christ's rule with the freedom we associate with democracy. Democratic freedom to do whatever we want is not the same thing as the spiritual freedom to become the people we were created to be. What is more, Jesus was not democratically elected to his position as Lord. God appointed him to that post. We may be cooperative or uncooperative followers, but we cannot vote him out of office. We cannot accurately describe Christ's rule with terms like "president" or "chief executive officer." Jesus is Lord.

For Christians to say that Jesus is Lord is not, however, only about politics. It is also something very personal. To say Jesus is Lord is an affirmation that in Christ we have found the source of life and the ground of our being. It is a testimony both to our own dependence and to God's provision. It is our way of saying "yes" to Christ's invitation to follow him, to obey him, and to be his disciples. The confession that Jesus is Lord acknowledges the fact that virtually all of us are in bondage to something—to wealth, or power, or pleasure, or fear, or whatever—and that it is precisely our submission to Christ that frees us and protects us from these other "lords" that would dominate our time and energy. As Jesus explained, the yoke of God's rule is "light" (Matthew 11:28-30), and it is empowering.

Just before his ascension, Jesus gathered his followers together and promised them that he would not leave them stranded in the world, but would send the Holy Spirit to guide them and empower them for the work of the gospel and the Christian life (John 14:15-19; Galatians 5:22-25). At the Jewish festival of Pentecost, ten days after Jesus' ascension, his disciples were together in Jerusalem for prayer when the promised Holy Spirit came upon them. As recounted in Acts 2, the Spirit entered the room with the sound of a mighty rushing wind, and tongues of fire appeared above each person's head. At that moment, the church came into existence, and this newly formed church would soon understand itself as the continuing "body of Christ" on earth. Membership in this body was not limited to any racial or ethnic group, but was open to everyone. People from everywhere responded. Soon the gospel message was being preached throughout the Roman Empire as well as in Africa, Asia, and Europe. As people responded, they too were being filled with the Holy Spirit. This same Holy Spirit sent from Jesus is in the world today, comforting us in our times of trouble and empowering us to proclaim good news and do good to all those who cross our paths.

Questions for Discussion

- When you hear the word "lord," what comes to mind?

- How is Jesus' lordship similar to, yet different from, other claims to authority?

- What do we gain by calling Jesus "Lord"? What risks do we run in using (or not using) this language?

- Who is the Holy Spirit? What does the Holy Spirit do?

What the Bible Says

(Luke 2:11) To you is born this day in the city of David a Savior, who is the Messiah, the Lord.

(Luke 6:46-48) Why do you call me 'Lord, Lord,' and do not do what I tell you? I will show you what someone is like who comes to me, hears my words, and acts on them. That one is like a man building a house, who dug deeply and laid the foundation on rock; when a flood arose, the river burst against that house but could not shake it, because it had been well built.

(Matthew 28:18-20) And Jesus came and said to [the disciples], "All authority in heaven and on earth has been given to me. Go therefore and make disciples of all nations, baptizing them in the name of the Father and of the Son and of the Holy Spirit, and teaching them to obey everything that I have commanded you.

And remember, I am with you always, to the end of the age."

(Luke 24:51) While he was blessing them, he withdrew from them and was carried up into heaven.

(Acts 1:8; 2:1-4) "But you will receive power when the Holy Spirit has come upon you; and you will be my witnesses in Jerusalem, in all Judea and Samaria, and to the ends of the earth." ... When the day of Pentecost had come, they were all together in one place. And suddenly from heaven there came a sound like the rush of a violent wind, and it filled the entire house where they were sitting. Divided tongues, as of fire, appeared among them, and a tongue rested on each of them. All of them were filled with the Holy Spirit and began to speak in other languages, as the Spirit gave them ability.

(Ephesians 1:20-23) God put this power to work in Christ when he raised him from the dead and seated him at his right hand in the heavenly places, far above all rule and authority and power and dominion, and above every name that is named, not only in this age but also in the age to come. And he has put all things under his feet and has made him the head over all things for the church, which is his body, the fullness of him who fills all in all.

What Our Creeds Say

(Apostles' Creed) I believe ... in Jesus Christ, God's only Son, Our Lord ... he ascended into heaven, he is seated at the right hand of the Father.

(Nicene Creed) We believe in one Lord, Jesus Christ ... he ascended to heaven and is seated at the right hand of the Father. He will come again in glory to judge the living and the dead, and his kingdom will have no end. We believe in the Holy Spirit, the Lord, the giver of life, who proceeds from the Father and the Son.

(Augsburg Confession III) Christ ... ascended into heaven, and sits on the right hand of God, that he may eternally rule and have dominion over all creatures, that through the Holy Spirit he may sanctify, purify, strengthen, and comfort all who believe in him, that he may bestow on them life and every grace and blessing, and that he may protect and defend them against the devil and against sin. The same Lord Christ will return openly to judge the living and the dead.

(Heidelberg Catechism) Q. 46 How do you understand the words: "He ascended into heaven"?
A. That Christ was taken up from the earth into heaven before the eyes of his disciples and remains there on our behalf until he comes again to judge the living and the dead.
Q. 50 Why is there added: "And sits at the right hand of God"?
A. Because Christ ascended into heaven so that he might manifest himself there as the Head of his Church, through whom the Father governs all things.
Q. 53 What do you believe concerning "the Holy Spirit?"
A. First, that, with the Father and the Son, he is God; second, that God's Spirit is also given equally eternal to me, preparing me through a true faith to share in

Christ and all his benefits, that he comforts me and will abide with me forever.

(Evangelical Catechism) Q. 73.4 To what purpose did he redeem you?
A. [Christ redeemed me] that I might be his own, live under him in his kingdom, and serve him in everlasting righteousness, innocence, and blessedness, even as he is risen from the dead, lives and reigns in all eternity.

What Our Liturgies Say—from the *UCC Book of Worship* (1986):

(Word and Sacrament I, Prayer for Mercy A, p. 38) Lord, have mercy; Christ, have mercy; Lord have mercy!

(Service of Word and Sacrament I, Act of Praise A, p. 39) Lord Jesus Christ, God's only begotten one, Lord God, Lamb of God, you take away the sin of the world: have mercy on us; you are seated at the right hand of Majesty; receive our prayer.

(Word and Sacrament I, Preface B, p. 46) We praise you that Jesus now reigns with you in glory and ever lives to pray for us.

(Brief Order for One Who Is Sick, p. 92) We rejoice that in a perfect victory over the grave you raised Christ with power to become sovereign in your realm.

(Committal, Prayers A, pp. 389-390) Keep us in everlasting communion with all who wait for you on earth and all who are with you in heaven, where Christ reigns with you and the Holy Spirit, ever one God, for ever and ever.

What Our Songs Say—from the *New Century Hymnal*:

(#257, Alleluia! Gracious Jesus!) Alleluia! Gracious Jesus! Yours the scepter, yours the throne! ... Not as orphans are we left in sorrow now ... Though the cloud from sight receive you when the forty days were o'er, shall our hearts forget your promise, "I am with you evermore."

(#258, Christ, Enthroned in Heavenly Splendor) Christ enthroned in heavenly splendor, first begotten from the dead, You alone, our strong defender, now lift up your people's head. Alleluia! Alleluia! Alleluia! Christ, our true and living Bread.

(#265, Come, O Spirit, with Your Sound) Come, O Spirit, with your sound like a wind, quick rushing; come from heaven, stir our hearts, each disciple touching! Mold our actions to your will, you our service giving; move in our community, transform now our living!

(#573, Lead On Eternal Sovereign) Lead on eternal Sovereign, we follow in your way; loud rings your cry for justice, your call for peace this day: Through prayerful preparation, your grace will make us strong, to carry on the struggle to triumph over wrong.

Themes for Reflection

Whom Do You Obey?: Many early Christians faced martyr-dom for claiming "Jesus is Lord." In their historical context, this affirmation meant "Caesar is not Lord" and that is why they were persecuted. Roman rulers claimed divinity, but many Christians would not offer them the ritual worship they demanded. Nor would they obey orders not to teach about Jesus. As Peter told the council in Jerusalem, "We must obey God rather than any human authority" (Acts 5:29). What would that kind of obedience to God look like today? How do we follow Jesus' commands and example? Discerning this is a task for the church in every generation and in every culture. The Evangelical Catechism says we live under Christ "in his kingdom, and serve him in ever-lasting righteousness, innocence, and blessedness." We are called to obey the Lord who has given himself for us and who desires fullness of life for us and all people.

Witnessing to and Working for God's Kingdom: A large part of following Jesus as Lord is to pray and work for the coming kingdom of God. The Evangelical Catechism says, "The mission of the Church is to extend the Kingdom of God, that is, to lead people to Christ and to establish Christian principles in every relation of life." Thus our lives include bearing witness to Jesus and continuing his work in the world by preaching, forgiving sins, working for justice, serving the needy, praying for one another, and so on. This calls for active participation on our part. Indeed, our work is grounded in our confidence that Jesus' rule enables our efforts to contribute to God's purposes. God's kingdom has not yet been fully realized. While we await God's final vic-tory, we must take evil seriously, but we must not take it more seriously than God's promise of the kingdom. By God's grace, we are called to persevere with hope in God's coming kingdom even when the immediate future seems frightening or unpromising.

The Holy Spirit Empowers Us: We are not called to achieve fullness of life on our own nor are we told we can resist the powers and temptations of evil unaided. Instead, Christ gives us the Holy Spirit as our comforter and help. The empowerment of the Holy Spirit is necessary for the transformation of our lives; it is necessary if we are to live according to the model Christ has set for us. Who is the Holy Spirit? The common Christian tradition shared by Protestants, Catholics, and Orthodox Christians alike is that the Holy Spirit is the third person of the Trinity, equal in status and power with God the Father and God the Son. The work of the Holy Spirit on earth is twofold. First, according to the Nicene Creed, the Holy Spirit is "the Lord, the giver of life." In other words, the Spirit is the source of life in all its fullness wherever it is found. Second, the Holy Spirit also continues and fulfills the work of Christ in our lives. Thus the Evangelical Catechism says, "The Holy Spirit makes known to us the call of God to come to Christ; he teaches us how, because of our sin, we need Christ; he leads us by repentance and faith to accept and follow Christ; he enables us thus to begin and live the new life of a child of God." The Westminster Confession adds that we ourselves bear the responsibility of opening our lives to the influence of the Spirit, cautioning believers to be "diligent in stirring up the grace of God that is in [us]." Some Christian traditions, such as Pentecostalism, put great emphasis on the extraordinary and unusual work of the Spirit, focusing on things like miraculous healings or speaking in tongues. Other traditions, the UCC among them, tend to focus less on the spectacular and more on the way the Spirit affects us as persons, prompting within us the attitudes identified by Paul as the "fruit" of the Spirit: "love, joy, peace, patience, kindness, generosity, faithfulness, gentleness, and self-control" (Galatians 5:22-23).

Questions for Discussion

- What "lords" other than Jesus clamor for our attention and loyalty?

- What does it mean to pledge our loyalty to Christ rather than to our family or our local community or our nation?

- Have there been times in your own life when you have made a conscious decision to follow Jesus rather than follow some other "lord"? Share this experience with the group.

- What does it mean to witness to and work for the kingdom of God? What do you have in mind when you pray for God's kingdom to come and God's will to be done on earth as in heaven?

- How have you experienced the Holy Spirit in your own life? How have you seen the Spirit work in someone else's life? How would you describe your relationship with the Holy Spirit?

- How would you explain the "good news" of recognizing Jesus as Lord to a friend, a neighbor, or a child? How would you explain the "good news" of submitting one's life to the guidance of the Holy Spirit?

Prayer

Leader: Lord, have mercy on us.

People: Lord, have mercy on us.

Leader: Christ, have mercy on us.

People: Christ, have mercy on us.

Leader: Lord, have mercy on us.

People: Lord, have mercy on us.

ALL: By what name shall we call you? You, our God, have been known by many names. We know that no one acclamation is adequate. We pray that you will hear us when we call from our hearts. It is in our hearts that your Spirit rules. You are able to hear the groanings of our hearts even when we have no words for them. We come alive in your Spirit, who enables us to move from prayer to praise to action. When the world clamors for our attention, make us attentive to your Spirit, that we may remain strong and faithful in you, and only you. Amen.

Chapter 8

Looking Ahead:
"Christ Will Come Again"

You promise ... eternal life in your realm
which has no end.

The New Testament concludes with the Revelation of Saint John who assures his readers that Christ will come again. This book tells us that believers should not only anticipate this coming, they should also pray for it. "Surely I am coming soon. Amen. Come, Lord Jesus!" (Revelation 22:20). The Bible offers suggestive hints, but does not give us full information about the exact method or timing of Christ's return. It does however inform us that Jesus, some day, will come again to rule the earth in justice and righteousness. Christ's return will transform both human life and the creation as a whole in such a way that everyone and everything will be re-formed according to God's purposes and design.

In conjunction with the resurrection of the dead, the return of Christ represents God's final and complete victory over sin, death, and evil. Christ's love will triumph over hate. His peace will supersede all conflict and anxiety. Christ's power to heal and liberate will procure permanent release from illness and bondage for God's people. "Death will be no more; mourning and crying and pain will be no more, for the first things have passed away" (Revelation 21:4). The catastrophe that has been known as sin, as well as all its effects, will be eliminated. Christ, the triumphant ruler, will re-configure life so that it is free of all division, conflict, hate, and separation.

One of the most important biblical passages dealing with the future is the prayer that Jesus taught his disciples to pray. This prayer asks for God's kingdom to come and God's will to be done on earth as it is in heaven. That is our hope. As mere creatures, we know that we do not have the power within ourselves to make God's kingdom present on earth. Yet, we also know that we are called to enact what we pray for. Thus our hope in the return of Christ is expressed in work for forgiveness, peace, justice, human dignity, and liberation right now, when and where we live.

The purpose of the biblical witness concerning the return of Christ is neither to frighten us nor to give us the details of how the future will unfold. Instead, the promise of Christ's return is meant to give us hope. Christ once told his disciples that he was going ahead of them to prepare a place for them in his Father's house (John 14:2-3). Christ is indeed in our future, but Christ is also in our present and in our past. He is the Alpha and the Omega, the beginning and the end. He broke into human life in a very special way as the incarnate Son of God. He breaks into our lives today through the Holy Spirit. He is the always-present God whenever we gather around the communion table or when-ever two or three are gathered in his name. Christ is also constantly breaking into our future, drawing the entire world toward the life God meant for us all to live.

We live in times of tension and violence. Terrorism stalks the world. Warfare is common. What is the place of hope in these conditions? Hope is not the same as simple optimism. Optimism is a passive attitude toward life. By contrast, hope is active. Hope works for what it hopes for. But hope can be hard to maintain when the world seems dark and the forces of chaos and evil seem to be rising rather than fading away. Christ has not promised that the path toward God's coming kingdom of justice, peace, and righteousness will emerge smoothly with no setbacks along the way. All we know is that eventually, in the end, God's will will be done. Our job in the present is to make sure we always include hope along with faith and love in our Christian living. By binding faith, hope, and love together we help to bring the kingdom of God closer—a kingdom that Christ has promised he himself will establish in its fullness when he returns.

Questions for Discussion

- We affirm in worship that Christ will come again. What does this mean?

- Early Christians frequently used the Aramaic word *maranatha* (meaning "our Lord, come") in their prayers saying, "Maranatha, Lord Jesus." Do you ever pray for Christ's return?

- What would characterize God's perfect world?

What the Bible Says

(Matthew 24:30-31, 36, 42) Then the sign of the Son of Man will appear in heaven, and then all the tribes of the earth will mourn, and they will "see the Son of Man coming on the clouds of heaven" with power and great glory. And he will send out his angels with a loud trumpet call, and they will gather his elect from the four winds, from one end of heaven to the other.... But about that day and hour no one knows, neither the angels of heaven, nor the Son, but only the Father. ... Keep awake therefore, for you do not know on what day your Lord is coming.

(Romans 8:18-21) I consider that the sufferings of this present time are not worth comparing with the glory about to be revealed to us. For the creation waits with eager longing for the revealing of the children of God; for the creation was subjected to futility, not of its own will but by the will of the one who subjected it, in hope that the creation itself will be set free from its bondage to decay and will obtain the freedom of the glory of the children of God.

(Revelation 1:8) "I am the Alpha and the Omega," says the Lord God, "who is and who was and who is to come, the Almighty."

(Revelation 22:20) The one who testifies to these things says, "Surely I am coming soon." Amen. Come, Lord Jesus!

(Jeremiah 29:11) For surely I know the plans I have for you, says the Lord, plans for your welfare and not for harm, to give you a future with hope.

What Our Creeds Say

(Apostles' Creed) [Jesus Christ] will come to judge the living and the dead. I believe in ... the resurrection of the body, and the life everlasting.

(Nicene Creed) He will come again in glory to judge the living and the dead, and his kingdom will have no end. ... We look for the resurrection of the dead and the life of the world to come.

(Heidelberg Catechism) Q. 52 What comfort does the return of Christ "to judge the living and the dead" give you?
A. That in all affliction and persecution I may await with head held high the very Judge from heaven who has already submitted himself to the judgment of God for me and has removed all the curse from me; that he will cast all his enemies and mine into everlasting condemnation, but he shall take me, together with all his elect, to himself into heavenly joy and glory.

(Westminster Confession XXXIII.i) God hath appointed a day wherein he will judge the world in righteousness by Jesus Christ, to whom all power and judgment is given of the Father. In which day ... all persons, that have lived upon earth, shall appear before the tribunal of Christ, to give an account of their thoughts, words, and deeds; and to receive according to what they have done in the body, whether good or evil.

What Our Liturgies Say—from the *UCC Book of Worship* (1986):

(Word and Sacrament I, II, Memorial Proclamation B, pp. 47, 71) Christ has died, Christ is risen, Christ will come again.

(Word and Sacrament II, Memorial Proclamation A, p. 71) By eating this bread and drinking this cup, we proclaim Christ's death, celebrate Christ's resurrection, and await Christ's coming again.

(Palm Sunday, Prayer, p. 188) … that united with Christ and all the faithful we may one day enter in triumph the city not made by human hands, the new Jerusalem, eternal in the heavens, where with you and the Holy Spirit, Christ lives in glory for ever.

(Lent, General Prayer, p. 493) As we who have been baptized into Jesus Christ enter into the life of the world, may we die with Christ that we may also rise with Christ. May we take part in your work of suffering and redeeming love, lifting up the oppressed, binding the brokenhearted, challenging the powerful, drawing all into a community of love.

What Our Songs Say—from the *New Century Hymnal*:

(#46, Hope of the World) Hope of the world, O Christ, o'er death victorious, who by this sign did conquer grief and pain, We would be faithful to your gospel glorious; our Sovereign who forever more shall reign!

(#403, My Hope Is Built on Nothing Less) When Christ shall come with trumpet sound, oh, may I then in Love be found, Dressed in God's righteousness alone, faultless to stand before the throne.

(#152, Born in the Night, Mary's Child) Hope of the world, Mary's Child, you're coming soon to reign; Sovereign of earth, Mary's Child, walk in our streets again.

(#608, Christ Will Come Again) Christ will come again, and joy shall be complete as flames of lightning love bedeck the judgment seat: then let us passionately

104

share the whole great gospel here on earth, until all things attain their end, when Christ shall come again.

Themes for Reflection

Eternal Life: Christians trust Christ's promise of life beyond this world (John 4:14). Jesus told his disciples that in his Father's house there are many dwelling places (John 14:2). Heaven is, however, not just a place, but also a way of life (Revelation 21:3-4). More than an entity in space or time, heaven is a relationship with God and others. It is the promise of the good news to those who have life in Christ. By contrast, the Bible says that hell and final destruction (however we understand those terms) are possibilities for those who reject the gift of life that God offers (Matthew 5:22, 23:33; Revelation 18). The choice is stark, but God wants everyone to choose life and not to choose the way of death that leads to hell (2 Peter 3:9). The vision of heaven that is revealed in John's Revelation is an affirmation that the grace and blessing of Christ that we have begun to experience in this world will be experienced in all its unending fullness in the world that is to come.

The Final Judgment: The Bible includes many references to God's coming in judgment. The Christian hope related to the final judgment is not focused on the vengeance of God, but on the loving judgment that sets things right. This judgment, grounded in Christ's death and resurrection, is God's final and incontestable "No!" to all evil and wrong, including that which we ourselves have done. While our creeds and confessions acknowledge that each of us will come under this judgment, they also assert that the judge is none other than Jesus himself who, as the Heidelberg Catechism puts it, "has already stood trial in my place before God and so has removed the whole curse from me." People will be judged by God's grace as revealed in the life and work of

Christ. Jesus manifested a way of life that was obedient to the Father's will and that was lived in full trust in God's love. It was a way of life that demonstrated humility and service to others. Judgment is God's activity of establishing justice without ever gloating over those who are judged or expressing glee over anyone's demise (Matthew 25:31-46; Philippians 2:5-11).

Could We Be Left Behind?: Many Christians today are convinced that the world is getting worse and worse and there is nothing we can do to change that. Their hope for the future is that Christ will return to earth to secretly rapture all true believers (themselves included) out of the world, lifting them up to heaven in an instant. Those who are left behind after this rapture will experience untold horrors as a seven-year period of tribulation begins. At the end of those seven years, Christ will return to earth yet again to destroy all his enemies and to inaugurate a thousand-year reign of God called the Millennium. The popular *Left Behind* novel series follows this way of thinking that was first developed in the 1820s by an English minister named John Nelson Darby. Many of our forbears in the UCC, and most UCC churches today, have rejected this vision of the future partly because it involves a very convoluted way of interpreting the Bible. It can also distract us from working for peace, justice, and the improvement of the world. Further, its vision of God as violent conqueror simply does not ring true to the God revealed in and through Jesus Christ. Our confessional statements have instead focused much more on the traditional concerns of Christ's return, the resurrection of the dead, judgment, and eternal life.

Questions for Discussion

- What role does hope regarding the future play in your life as a Christian?

- How does your understanding of Christ's coming again connect with your understanding of Christ's resurrection and ascension?

- Is there a connection between your understanding of Christ's coming again and your understanding of Christ being present in the Word and sacraments?

- What do you think eternal life in heaven might look like?

- What do you fear or hope for in relation to God's final judgment on your life?

- Have you read any of the *Left Behind* novels? What do you think of their claim that some Christians will be "raptured" out of the world before Christ returns and that a period of great tribulation will follow that rapture?

- How does belief in the return of Christ affect your attitude toward life today?

- How would you explain the "good news" of Christ's future return to a friend, a neighbor, or a child?

Prayer

Dear God, in Jesus you taught us to pray for your will to be done on earth. We still struggle to understand what that means. We believe that you have called us and claimed us as your own. We believe that your call and promise are for all people. Empower us to share this good news with those around us. While we live here, in this place and time, remind us that we also live in you, in your time ripe with salvation, which cannot be measured by earthly means. Your will be done. Your will be done on earth as in heaven. When we do not understand your time and your ways, then teach us to trust that we will live with you forever, even as your children before us have trusted. Our hope is in you, through Christ and the Holy Spirit. Amen.

Chapter 9

Christ's Life Flows into the Church: "You Call, You Promise"

You call us into your church to accept the
cost and joy of discipleship,
to be your servants in the service of others,
to proclaim the gospel to all the world
and resist the powers of evil,
to share in Christ's baptism and eat at his table,
to join him in his passion and victory.
You promise to all who trust you forgiveness of sins and
fullness of grace, courage in the struggle
for justice and peace,
your presence in trial and rejoicing,
and eternal life in your realm which has no end.

The previous chapters have concentrated on what the UCC Statement of Faith says about Christ. In this final chapter, we focus instead on the implications of those beliefs for how we live as followers of Jesus. Each of the previous chapters has already raised some of the more practical questions about life. What we consider here is the broader pattern of how who Christ is shapes the way of life to which Christ calls us. The UCC Statement of Faith actually has a good deal to say in this regard, and thus this is a fitting way to end our study.

As Jesus began his earthly ministry, he called disciples to follow him and to participate in his work. He told fishermen that they would now "fish for people" (Matthew 4:18-22). Jesus himself went about overcoming the destructive forces of sin, illness, and death and inaugurating God's new kingdom based on justice and forgiveness, and he sent out his disciples to do the same. The Gospel of Luke records that while Jesus was still on earth he dispatched his followers to heal the sick and preach the kingdom of God, and they came back rejoicing (Luke 10:1-20). Later, after Jesus' death, resurrection, and ascension, the disciples were specifically charged with the task of spreading the gospel and baptizing people in the name of the Father, Son, and Holy Spirit (Matthew 28:18-20). They were also to attend to the human needs of church members and others. This is all part of what is sometimes called the "Great Commission."

This great commission extends to us as well. We are called, by God, into the church (the body of Christ), which has the task of continuing Christ's work in the world. Jesus calls each of us to put our lives at his disposal to expand God's kingdom and share his healing and redeeming love in the world in which we live. Wherever there is injustice, hunger, illness, or human need, Christians are to actively seek justice and wholeness. We are to resist evil in whatever guise it is found. We are also to be joyful. Our proclamation, like Christ's, is that "the kingdom of heaven has come near" (Matthew 10:7). We are to bear witness that "Christ Jesus came into the world to save sinners" (1 Timothy 1:15). Through Jesus, all people may be drawn into personal and loving relationship with the Father, Son, and Holy Spirit, for God seeks "to save all people from aimlessness and sin," as our Statement of Faith puts it.

We do not fulfill this call on our own; we share it with Christ. Much as family rituals shape us as we grow, so the rituals of the church show us what to do as they simultane-ously empower us to do it. In worship, we rehearse the life we are called to live in the world. Take baptism as an example. When we are baptized, we are buried (or drowned) with Christ, so that "just as Christ was raised from the dead by the glory of the Father, so we too might walk in newness of life" (Romans 6:4). In baptism, we are sacramentally identified with Christ's death and resurrection, and then we are expected to act accordingly in the world. We are called truly to be dead to pride and envy and to hatred and spite, and we are called to be fully alive to love, peace, justice, patience, and compassion. The gift of new life and identity we receive as children of God is the result of Christ's own passion and victory.

In communion or the Eucharist, we see the same thing. The broken bread and poured out wine symbolize and in some sense make present Christ's death for our sakes. The Last Supper, on which communion is based, was also a harbinger of the final feast we will share with all the saints when Christ returns to make all things new. As we live our lives within the world, the Eucharistic celebration thus calls us to allow ourselves to be broken for others. It calls us to share our resources—our bread and wine that symbolize the basic needs of humankind—with those in need. It also calls us to live our lives in light of the joy that will be part of the eternal festival that is heaven, where we will someday spend eternity with God.

The Statement of Faith lists promises in which we hear, once again, the themes we have already discussed about Christ himself. Because of Christ, we are promised forgiveness of sins and a full measure of God's favor—the very things we are unable to merit or accomplish on our own. We are also promised courage and strength for the difficult work of justice and peace—courage and strength that, once, again, we cannot manufacture on our own. The challenge before us is immense, and our calling exceeds our natural abilities, but Christ is alive and through the Holy Spirit, we are given the grace to undertake what we could never even begin on our own.

This study has spent a good deal of time focusing on ideas. It is a theological study of the life and significance of Christ. But theology should never be a matter of ideas alone. Instead, theology should help us understand and experience God, allowing our lives to be changed so that we become better disciples of Christ. That is our calling and that is our responsibility. But our responsibility is always matched, indeed exceeded, by the promise that because of Christ and in Christ God will never leave us. Christ is Emmanuel—God with us—and when God is with us, supporting us and empowering us for faith, hope, and love, we truly can live as the redeemed sinners Christ has allowed us to become.

Discussion Questions

- What are some of the ways you see the church continuing the work of Christ in the world?

- Some congregations renew their baptismal vows from time to time. Is this a practice in your congregation? How do you remember your baptismal identification with Christ?

- How does your congregation understand what happens in the Lord's Supper? Is Christ seen as being actually present in the bread and wine? Is communion simply a way of reminding us of Christ's death 2,000 years ago? What goes through your mind during the celebration of Holy Communion?

- Of all of God's promises to you, which ones do you rely on most strongly?

What the Bible Says

(Mark 8:34) If any want to become my followers, let them deny themselves and take up their cross and follow me. For those who want to save their life will lose it, and those who lose their life for my sake, and for the sake of the gospel, will save it.

(Luke 9:1-2) Then Jesus called the twelve together and gave them power and authority over all demons and to cure diseases, and he sent them out to proclaim the kingdom of God and to heal.

(John 13:12-17) After [Jesus] had washed [his disciples'] feet, had put on his robe, and had returned to the table, he said to them, "Do you know what I have done to you? You call me Teacher and Lord—and you are right, for that is what I am. So if I, your Lord and Teacher, have washed your feet, you also ought to wash one another's feet. For I have set you an example, that you also should do as I have done to you. Very truly, I tell you, servants are not greater than their master, nor are messengers greater than the one who sent them. If you know these things, you are blessed if you do them."

(John 17:21-23) As you, Father, are in me and I am in you, may they also be in us, so that the world may believe that you have sent me. The glory that you have given me I have given them, so that they may be one, as we are one, I in them and you in me, that they may become completely one, so that the world may know that you have sent me and have loved them even as you have loved me.

(1 Corinthians 12:27) Now you are the body of Christ and individually members of it.

(Romans 6:3-5) Do you not know that all of us who have been baptized into Christ Jesus were baptized into his death? Therefore we have been buried with him by baptism into death, so that, just as Christ was raised from the dead by the glory of the Father, so we too might walk in newness of life. For if we have been united with him in a death like his, we will certainly be united with him in a resurrection like his.

(1 Corinthians 11:23-26) For I received from the Lord what I also handed on to you, that the Lord Jesus on the night when he was betrayed took a loaf of bread, and when he had given thanks, he broke it and said, "This is my body that is for you. Do this in remembrance of me." In the same way he took the cup also, after supper, saying, "This cup is the new covenant in my blood. Do this, as often as you drink it, in remembrance of me." For as often as you eat this bread and drink the cup, you proclaim the Lord's death until he comes.

(1 Peter 2:4-5, 9-10) Come to him, a living stone, though rejected by mortals yet chosen and precious in God's sight, and like living stones, let yourselves be built into a spiritual house, to be a holy priesthood, to offer spiritual sacrifices acceptable to God through Jesus Christ ... But you are a chosen race, a royal

priesthood, a holy nation, God's own people, in order that you may proclaim the mighty acts of him who called you out of darkness into his marvelous light.

What Our Creeds Say

(Apostles' Creed) I believe in the Holy Spirit, the holy catholic Church, the communion of saints, the forgiveness of sins, the resurrection of the body, and the life everlasting.

(Heidelberg Catechism) Q. 1 What is your only comfort, in life and in death?
A. That I belong—body and soul, in life and in death—not to myself but to my faithful Savior, Jesus Christ, who at the cost of his own blood has fully paid for all my sins and has completely freed me from the dominion of the devil; that he protects me so well that without the will of my Father in heaven not a hair can fall from my head; indeed, that everything must fit his purpose for my salvation. Therefore, by his Holy Spirit, he also assures me of eternal life, and makes me wholeheartedly willing and ready from now on to live for him.
Q. 32 But why are you called a Christian?
A. Because through faith I share in Christ and thus in his anointing, so that I may confess his name, and offer myself a living sacrifice of gratitude to him, and fight against sin and the devil with a free and good conscience throughout this life and hereafter rule with him in eternity over all creatures.
Q. 65 Since, then, faith alone makes share in Christ and all his benefits, where does such faith originate?
A. The Holy Spirit creates it in our hearts by the

preaching of the holy gospel, and confirms it by the use of the holy Sacraments.

(Westminster Confession XXVI.i) All saints that are united to Jesus Christ their head, by his Spirit and by faith, have fellowship with him in his graces, sufferings, death, resurrection, and glory: and being united to one another in love, they have communion in each other's gifts and graces, and are obliged to the performance of such duties, public and private, as do conduce to their mutual good, both in the inward and the outward man.

(Evangelical Catechism) Q. 88 Why is the church called "one" Church?
A. The Christian Church is called the "one" Church because it has one Lord, one faith, one baptism, one God and Father of all, as it is written in Ephesians 4:3-6: Giving diligence to keep the unity of the Spirit in the bond of peace. There is one body, and one Spirit, even as also you were called in one hope of your calling; one Lord, one faith, one baptism, one God and Father of all, who is over all, and through all, and in all.
Q. 118 What does God do for us in Holy Baptism?
A. In Holy Baptism God imparts the gift of the new life unto man, receives him into his fellowship as his child, and admits him as a member of the Christian Church.
Q. 125 What is the Lord's Supper?
A. The Lord's Supper is the sacrament by which we receive the body and blood of our Lord Jesus Christ as the nourishment of our new life, strengthen the fellowship with Christ and all believers, and confess that he has died for us.

What Our Liturgies Say—from the *UCC Book of Worship* (1986):

(Word and Sacrament I, Commissioning, p. 53) Strengthen the fainthearted; support the weak; help the afflicted; honor all people; love and serve God, rejoicing in the power of the Holy Spirit.

(Baptism, Address B, pp. 135-136) Baptism is the sacrament through which we are united to Jesus Christ and given part in Christ's ministry of reconciliation. Baptism is the visible sign of an invisible event: the reconciliation of people to God. It shows the death of self and the rising to a life of obedience and praise. It shows also the pouring out of the Holy Spirit on those whom God has chosen. In baptism, God works in us the power of forgiveness, the renewal of the Spirit, and the knowledge of the call to be God's people always.

(Word and Sacrament II, Communion Prayer A, pp. 71-72) Through this meal, make us the body of Christ, the church, your servant people, that we may be salt, and light, and leaven for the furtherance of your will in all the world.

(Reception of Members, Questions of the Candidates, p. 161) Do you promise, by the grace of God, to be Christ's disciple, to follow in the way of our Savior, to resist oppression and evil, to show love and justice, and to witness to the work and word of Jesus Christ as best as you are able?

What Our Songs Say—from the *New Century Hymnal*:

(#324, Baptized into Your Name Most Holy) Baptized into your name most holy, O Father, Son, and Holy Ghost, I claim a place, though weak and lowly, Among your seed, your chosen host. Buried with Christ and dead to sin, I have your Spirit now within.

(#332, As We Gather at Your Table) As we gather at your table, as we listen to your word, help us know, O God, your presence; let our hearts and minds be stirred ... teach us through this holy banquet how to make Love's victory known. Turn our worship into witness in the sacrament of life; send us forth to love and serve you, bringing peace where there is strife.

(#387, O Christ, the Great Foundation) O Christ, the great foundation on which your people stand to preach your true salvation in every age and land ... Where tyrants' hold is tightened, where strong devour the weak, where innocents are frightened, the righteous fear to speak, There let your church awaking attack the powers of sin and, all their ramparts breaking, with you the victory win.

(#457, Jesus, I Live to You) Jesus, I live to you, the loveliest and best; My life will be your life in me, in your blessed love I rest.

(#498, Jesu, Jesu, Fill Us with Your Love) Jesu, Jesu, fill us with your love, show us how to serve the neighbors we have from you. These are the ones we should serve, these are the ones we should love; all these are neighbors to us and you. Loving puts us on our knees, showing our faith by our deeds, serving the neighbors we have from you.

Themes for Reflection

Font, Pulpit, Pew, and Table: Look around your sanctuary. The furnishings there show key features of the shared life of those whom God calls and to whom God makes gracious promises. At the font, one is incorporated into the body of Christ. Baptism is God's gift, bringing us into union with Christ, with each other, and with the church of every time and place. It is the sign and seal of our discipleship. From the pulpit, one hears the proclamation of the gospel. This reassures us that God has come to us in Christ and cultivates our faith and trust in God. It also names evils that must be resisted and challenges disciples to live Christ-formed lives. Here we are regularly reoriented to the faith we affirm. The pews (or chairs) stress that all of us are members of the body of Christ. Worship services need worshipers, not just worship leaders. God's call and promise are for each one of us. The table provides spiritual food for the spiritual journey of discipleship, renewing Christ's life in us. Here we proclaim Christ's death and resurrection and look forward to his coming again.

Missionary Endeavor: From the earliest days of the church, Christians have believed that the good news of Christ is for all people. It is a message that should go to everyone. As Jesus himself told his disciples after his resurrection, "you will by my witnesses in Jerusalem, in Judea and Samaria, and to the ends of the earth" (Acts 1:8). Within a hundred years of Christ's death, the Christian message had been preached throughout the Roman Empire and as far away as India. Since that time, the spread of the gospel has gone forward in fits and starts. Western Europe was evangelized during the first millennium at the same time that

Orthodoxy was expanding into Eastern Europe and Central Asia. Later, the Americas would be evangelized along with East Asia. More recently, Christianity has spread widely in Africa. In its work of evangelism, the church has had a mixed record, sometimes using violence or collusion with colonial exploitation to advance the message of Christ. Despite those flaws, the gospel has taken root and flourished around the world, so that now a third of the world's population is Christian. We can no longer allow cultural prejudices or economic gain to deform the ways in which we share Christ's message with others. The challenge before us today is to preach and live the gospel around the world in a manner that truly reflects Christ's love and compassion for every human being.

Church Unity and Division: Our creeds and confessions affirm the oneness of the church, and yet a sense of unity often seems illusive. Today there are more different kinds of Christians than ever before—and there is more tension. Eastern and Western Christians who had been drifting apart for centuries officially split in 1054 into the Roman Catholic and Orthodox Churches. At the beginning of the sixteenth century, Protestant movements emerged and Western Christianity soon divided into five distinct streams—Lutheran, Reformed, Anglican, Anabaptist, and Roman Catholic—as well as a host of smaller rivulets. In our own day, denominations are dividing once again over such issues as biblical interpretation, sexuality, and worship styles. Yet, God calls us to unity, and even more than that to genuinely mutual love. When the United Church of Christ was formed, it hoped to be a catalyst for overcoming the many divisions within Christianity. It took as its motto "that they may all be one," a phrase from Jesus' prayer for the unity of the church (John 17:11). Full restoration of unity among the followers of Christ has not yet emerged, but it remains an integral part of our calling as the body of Christ. We serve one Lord. We have one message of love and forgiveness. We share one Holy Spirit who comforts and empowers us. Animated by God's promises, we need to find ways of making that unity real and visible. This is perhaps the greatest challenge facing the church today. How can we rightly honor Christ when we divide Christ and use our different visions of Christ to denounce each other? Some day we will all sing our praise of Christ in unison saying, "all blessing and honor, glory and power be unto you." Let us begin to practice that unity in Christ and with Christ right now.

Questions for Discussion

- How has your life been shaped by Christ?

- Do you think of yourself as belonging to the body of Christ? What does this image convey to you?

- What embarrassments or inconveniences do you suffer as Christ's disciple? What sacrifices do you make for the sake of Christ? How ready might you be to die for the sake of Christ?

- In what ways does being Christ's disciple bring you joy?

- How do you participate in the proclamation of the gospel? In the service of others? In the struggle for justice and peace?

- Reflect on times when you have experienced God's presence in times of trial or rejoicing. What was this like?

- What is the "good news" in being part of Christ's church? How would you explain that to a friend or neighbor or to a child?

Prayer

O God, Author of Life, you have called us and given us the privilege and the responsibility of being your body in our world. You claim us in the waters of baptism and feed us at your table. As your word is proclaimed, help us to hear your voice and discern the tasks you give us. Teach us, we pray, to love you and one another, even as Jesus taught us. Grant us joy in following Jesus, our Savior, and in embodying your will and work in our communities. May we become one in Christ. In Jesus' name. Amen.

Contributors

Anne T. Thayer (editor) is a lay member of Hamilton Park United Church of Christ in Lancaster, PA. She is the Paul and Minnie Diefenderfer Associate Professor of Mercersburg and Ecumenical Theology and Church History at Lancaster Theological Seminary and holds a Ph.D. from Harvard University. Recent book publications include: *Penitence in the Age of Reformations* (Ashgate, 2000) and *Penitence, Preaching and the Coming of the Reformation* (Ashgate, 2002).

Douglas Jacobsen (editor) is a layperson and has been a member of St. Paul's United Church of Christ in Mechanicsburg, PA, since 1986. He is Distinguished Professor of Church History and Theology at Messiah College (Grantham, PA) and holds a Ph.D. from the University of Chicago. Recent publications include: *Thinking in the Spirit: Theologies of the Early Pentecostal Movement* (Indiana University Press, 2003); *Scholarship and Christian Faith* (Oxford University Press, 2004); and *Gracious Christianity* (Baker Academic, 2006).

Marja L. Coons-Torn is the Conference Minister and President of Penn Central Conference, United Church of Christ. She was ordained in 1976 and has served churches in New Mexico, Illinois, New York and Montana, as well as serving as an Associate Conference Minister in the Indiana-Kentucky Conference. She received a Master of Divinity degree from Andover Newton Theological School in 1976 and a Doctor of Ministry degree from Eden Theological Seminary in 1994.

Tom Lush is pastor of Myerstown United Church of Christ in Myerstown, PA. He holds a D.Min. from Princeton Theological Seminary. Currently serving as chairperson of the Theological Commission of the Penn Central Conference, he has been a pastor in the Conference for 29 years.

Patricia Macneal graduated from Pomona College and was a Fulbright Scholar at the University of Munich (Germany). She joined St. Peter's United Church of Christ in Rebersburg in 1958, where she serves as organist. Her interest in Appalachia's traditional arts and culture and her concern for justice led her to organize Central Pennsylvania Village Crafts and the Northern Tier Cultural Alliance. She has co-authored two books, *Quilts from Appalachia* (1986) and *Headwaters and Hardwoods* (1997).

Judith C. Maust is a layperson and has been a member of Trinity United Church of Christ in Hanover, PA, since 1969. She is a Financial Administrator for a dental practice and a graduate of Gettysburg College.

David E. Roe is Senior Pastor of Shiloh United Church of Christ in York, PA. He graduated from Houghton College and Colgate Rochester Divinity School. He has also served churches in New York, Massachusetts, Ohio, and Indiana over the past 42 years.

Harry G. Royer, pastor of Trinity United Church of Christ, East Petersburg, PA, graduated from Franklin and Marshall College and the Lancaster Theological Seminary. He is one of the founders of the Order of Corpus Christi and the Mercersburg Society. He serves as a pastor preceptor at Lancaster Theological Seminary.

RELATED TITLES
FROM UNITED CHURCH PRESS

BELIEVING, CARING, AND DOING IN THE UNITED CHURCH OF CHRIST
An Interpretation
GABRIEL FACKRE
0-8298-1641-0 / paper / 256 pages / $20.00
Explores the "believing, caring, and doing" dimensions of the United Church of Christ and discusses the UCC's inter-relation of its theological orientation—as found in key texts, traditions, and movements—its ecumenical commitments, and its deeds of justice and peace.

CONFESSING OUR FAITH
An Interpretation of the Statement of Faith of the United Church of Christ
ROGER L. SHINN
0-8298-0866-3 / paper / 132 pages / $13.00
This resource includes the description of the process that led to the adoption of the Statement of Faith by the UCC in 1959.

THE EVOLUTION OF A UCC STYLE
Essays in the History, Ecclesiology, and Culture of the United Church of Christ
RANDI J. WALKER
0-8298-1493-0 / paper / 240 pages / $30.00
Focuses on the development of the themes that define the UCC: inclusiveness, diversity of theological heritage (Reformation, Enlightenment, and Pietism), congregational polity (the one and the many), a liberal theological approach, and ecumenical spirit.

FREEDOM WITH ORDER
The Doctrine of the Church in the United Church of Christ
ROBERT S. PAUL

0-8298-0749-7 / paper / 244 pages / $13.00
This book encourages a discussion of the doctrines of the UCC that will faithfully express the historical traditions and the ecumenical imperatives that formed the denomination.

PRISM
A Theological Forum for the United Church of Christ
LEE C. BARRETT III AND ELIZABETH C. NORDBECK, EDITORS
Published twice a year, Prism, a growing publication currently consisting of 20 issues, is sponsored by the seminaries of the United Church of Christ. As a journal for the whole church, its goal is to offer serious theological reflection from a diversity of viewpoints on issues of faith, mission, and ministry.
$12.00 for one-year subscription $20.00 for two-year subscription.

THEOLOGY AND IDENTITY
Traditions, Movements, and Polity in the United Church of Christ
Enlarged Edition
DANIEL L. JOHNSON AND CHARLES HAMBRICK-STOWE, EDS.
978-0-8298-1772-0 / paper / 240 pages / $20.00
This collection of essays spans the breadth of the United Church of Christ, from the perspective of its theological issues and movements.

WHO DO YOU SAY THAT I AM?
Christology and Identity in the United Church of Christ
SCOTT R. PAETH, EDITOR
978-0-8298-1702-7 / paper / 224 pages / $28.00
This collection of essays from theologians across the United Church of Christ spectrum focuses on the role of Christology— how it developed and the part it plays in shaping the direction and mission of the church.

UNITED AND UNITING
The Meaning of an Ecclesial Journey
LOUIS H. GUNNEMANN
0-8298-0757-8 / paper / 222 pages / $17.00
This book provides historical perspective and a call to recover the original vision for a greater understanding of the denomination.

UNITED CHURCH OF CHRIST
Who We Are, What We Believe
U3000 / paper / $0.30 each; $25.00 per 100
This popular leaflet interprets the UCC and is suitable for distribution to your congregation.

To order these or any other books from United Church Press, call or write to:
UNITED CHURCH PRESS 700 PROSPECT AVENUE CLEVELAND, OH 44115-1100
Phone orders: 800.537.3394 (M—F, 8:30 am—4:30 pm ET)
Fax orders: 216.736.2206
Please include shipping charges of $6 for the first book and 75¢ for each additional book.
Or order from our web site at www.unitedchurchpress.com
Prices *subject to change without notice.*